WHITETAILS

A Research Based Hunting Model

A. Robert Sheppard, M.D.

Table of Contents

Whitetails: A Research Based Hunting Model

A. Robert Sheppard, M.D.

Published by Robert Sheppard, 2010.

While every precaution has been taken in the preparation of this book, the publisher assumes no responsibility for errors or omissions, or for damages resulting from the use of the information contained herein.

WHITETAILS: A RESEARCH BASED HUNTING MODEL

First edition. May 1, 2010.

Written by A. Robert Sheppard, M.D..

Dedication

I am pleased to dedicate this book, the work of its production, the pursuits that brought it into being, and the time and research that made it possible to my family ...my wife, Brenda, our son, Dustin, and our daughter, Molly.

Acknowledgments

I first acknowledge my Lord and Savior, Jesus Christ, who through his grace, love, suffering, and death made a way for me to come to the Father when no other option was available. My intent is to honor him with every action I take.

I then acknowledge the concessions my family made to allow such a pursuit to take place in a single individual's life. My wife of more than thirty years remains my closest friend today. Our children remain our most intimate friends as well. They all not only sacrificed, but also shared and enjoyed much of my life's outdoor pursuits.

I must also acknowledge my friend and hunting buddy, Ronnie Groom. Ronnie, more so than any other, invited me into his inmost thoughts on hunting. He was and is a master of masters of the whitetail. I was slow to learn, but he is such a powerful and patient teacher, I was destined to double my knowledge many times under his direction.

My close friend and hunting buddy, David Stokes, made possible not only some of the finest hunting terrain the South has to offer literally out my backdoor, but he also shared these woods with the same passion to which I am accustomed.

My friends, Johnny Lanier and Leo Allen, the owners of Bent Creek Lodge have treated me like family, provided the business structure through which we could accomplish groundbreaking research on the whitetail, and I continue to hold a debt of gratitude to them as well.

To my longtime friend John Phillips, perhaps the most prolific outdoor writer in America for more than forty years, I owe a debt of gratitude for painstakingly helping me crawl then walk, then run and finally soar into the realm of the outdoor writer.

Foreword

Here is the book that is surely destined to become the definitive work on whitetail deer hunting. It is the result of Dr. Bob Sheppard's lifetime of diligently pursuing these magnificent creatures with a determination and persistence few of us can process. It is at once an entertaining novel, a textbook and a reference manual that you will find yourself going back to again and again.

Dr. Sheppard is not only the finest hunter any of us is likely to encounter; he is also one who is completely unselfish in sharing his insights with others. In short, he wants each of us to share in his love of the outdoors in general and whitetail hunting in particular, as well as in the success he has experienced in his impassioned pursuit. Fortunately for us, he is an extraordinarily gifted teacher—one who truly loves to teach others and one who is exceptionally good at it.

As he says in his book, it has never been enough for him to see that things happen, he has always wanted to know why they happen as they do. It is this analytical approach that enables him to bring his experiences to us in a way that we are better able to understand and effectively apply them in our whitetail pursuits. To have insight into why deer do certain things in certain ways at certain times will most assuredly make anyone a better hunter, especially when combined with detailed explanations of how to best utilize this insight.

If you are a beginning hunter, applying the knowledge to be gained from this book will greatly increase your chance of consistent success. Even the experienced hunter will begin to see so much in a new light—one that will translate into more hunting success and greater enjoyment from the process.

Before you begin to think that Dr. Sheppard's book begins and ends with hunting, rest assured that it is so much more. It is about the lessons learned from a life well lived. So sit back and enjoy the ride. Your thinking is sure to be challenged, but you will be glad you took the trip.
—David F. Stokes

Introduction

I grew up in the South, on a farm, the son of tenant farmers, and that simple heritage set the stage for much of my success and my ability to enjoy life. A piece from the invitation to my parent's sixtieth wedding anniversary offers a glimpse into that childhood.

> In this late hour of the twentieth century much is wrong with American families. Not often do married couples survive long enough to reach an aged wedding anniversary. More often than not, a lack of commitment rips families apart before the grip of death can fasten its hold. We are happy to share with you that the former has not yet taken either of our parents. We are even more pleased to tell you that their commitment to each other and to us, their three children, has been unfaltering and life long.
>
> They married during this country's deepest depression, young, penniless, and uneducated. Yet, their personal shortcomings knew no bounds. They scratched the earth with the tenacity

and vigor that made America great. They sacrificed deeply and unselfishly to assure their children had what they needed to face an adverse world. They taught us not only that God is real but that He is personal, sovereign, and loving. They lived the gospel message before us and their neighbors.

Historical Backdrop

This relentless, unyielding pursuit of efficiency and success my parents drilled into me at an early age gave me the competitive edge required to later enter one of the world's most competitive academic arenas to become a physician and from there to become a teaching professor in one of the world's largest medical schools. And indeed, it was a long and difficult pursuit of study, but I've told many in recent years that I spent more time attempting to learn the habits of the whitetail than I did preparing for the field of medicine. Most doubt that, and maybe it is an exaggeration...but not by much! Most of my childhood leisure days were spent fishing with my dad. If it swam, I wanted to catch it. And catch it I did. I became a very successful bluegill and bass fisherman before my teenage years had faded. College for me was four years of really focused grit. I worked full time and took a heavy course load, and not much time was left to hunt or catch anything beyond a never adequate nap. The work on the farm had left little time for reading, and by the time I entered college at the University of Alabama, I was nearly illiterate despite excellent high school grades. Early on in college, I discovered I had a mind for analytical things and did well in math, chemistry, physics, and biology disciplines. By the time I was a junior, I had struggled through the humanities with modest grades but had focused my course work on mostly the math and sciences ...because I had learned I could make A's in this analytical coursework. Still, I knew I had a major deficit in my skill with words and continued to work on my reading skills. A friend and roommate, Randy Coshatt, had given me a small dictionary early in my freshman year. As I struggled with reading the coursework, I held the paperback dictionary close at hand, highlighting each word I had to look up. When I was a senior at the University of Alabama, more than 80 percent of the words in the little paperback had been highlighted! Randy, I will never forget you buddy.

Like college, the four years in medical school were pretty demanding, but I was not yet satisfied with my command of the English language. In 1976, I began a writing career and for the ensuing ten years became a magazine editor and published more than 400 articles in most of America's outdoor magazines and earned memberships in the OWAA (Outdoor Writers Association of America) and SEOPA (Southeastern Outdoor Press Association). Remember, this was before the PC had hit the market. Writing, meant, well, just that...writing. To write an article, I hand wrote it, hand corrected it (usually four or five drafts), and then typed it up on a manual typewriter I had used from high school in the 1960s. Electric typewriters were available, but I couldn't afford one at that point in my career. But I got through it and by the late 1980s had adopted the PC (actually a Mac), even taught myself to program, and was more or less "educated." Finally! My college English professor would have been more dumbfounded than proud of me.

I should hope you will enjoy the content of this book as much as I have in writing it. Although its focus is on strategies for taking whitetails, it is a book about Bob Sheppard, his family, friends, life, and God. If a memory crossed my mind, I likely wrote about it. In doing so, I hoped to capture not only a fruitful lifetime of pursuing these magnificent creatures of creation, but also to sprinkle that Whitetails experience with elements of Southern American culture at the dawn of the twenty-first century.

My pursuit of the whitetail has taken a lifetime, and I continue to fine-tune those skills each season. However, I suspect as you will see, I have added an element of diligence, time, and analytical depth not common to the sport. It is one thing to be passionate. It is yet another to be analytical about that passion. Indeed, I have been fortunate enough to have a host of factors fall into place by sheer luck that most hunters can only dream about. More about that later as well.

15

My whitetail hunting is limited almost
exclusively to the Southeastern United States.
Most of the tactics, research, and conclusions I
draw will apply to the whitetail wherever he may
live but not with equal penetration. Having
hunted a few times in central Texas, for example,
I commented to the ranch manager after a few
days there, "If your whitetail herd should be
transplanted to Alabama, they would all be dead
by Thanksgiving!" By the same token, a few
years back I had invited some friends from Ohio
to come down to bow hunt with me. I took a
compass reading and walked off about a mile into
a 7,000-acre block of forested land. That evening
at supper, my Yankee friend asked, "How in the
world did you ever figure out where to hunt in
such a vast expanse of timber?" How, indeed!
Again, more about this later.

I must confess this book is more a result of
my wife, Brenda's diligence, sacrifice, hard
work, and patience than my own. She is the one
who put up with my dogged analytical fanaticism
...and still loves me after more than thirty-five
years of this stuff. She remains the love of my
life to this day. Our children, Dusty and Molly,
caught the bug early in life as well. I was such a
fanatic about deer hunting when Dust, as we call
him, was young that he became more enamored
with fishing than hunting. When he was about
four, I had him stashed safely in a sleeping bag in

the weeds at the edge of a large bean field I was glassing. It was cold, windy, and drizzling rain. I became engrossed in watching a nice eight-point working his way toward me from some distance away until I heard him sobbing. I crawled back to see what the problem might be. He was soaked and freezing!

Molly, on the other hand, was imprinted at the age of five. She was sitting with me in a ladder stand one cold morning at the end of a slough when two deer came slipping cautiously by us off to her side of the tree. I leaned into my .308 and said, "Hold your ears, Mollycule," as I call her. I squeezed the trigger. One of the deer hit the dirt from where it had stood, and the other bounded a few yards and stopped. She looked up at me through big blue eyes and said indignantly, "Well, shoot the other one, Daddy!" She's taken more monster whitetails than most men and still loves to hunt. These precious children remain two of my best friends to this day.

The Early Days

The area of southeast Alabama where I grew up had no whitetails when I was a child. In fact, it had no big game at all, only quail, squirrels, and a few doves. I was predominantly a fisherman through my childhood years, but I was happy in the woods or on the water, regardless of the pursuit. Although I began deer hunting in the late 1960s, shortly after arriving at college at the University of Alabama in Tuscaloosa, I continued to be frustrated with my efforts for many years. The region I hunted in west central Alabama was a farming district at that point in history (now a timber industry), and my hunting mostly consisted of glassing large bean fields to locate feeding whitetails. I was in a hunting club with some 300 members, and though we had abundant land to hunt, more than 30,000 acres, the club was a dog hunting club, and no "stalk hunting," as it was called, was allowed except during weekdays. Less than half a dozen of the club's 300 members hunted with a centerfire rifle. It was considered a very dangerous weapon and frowned upon by club members where the shotgun with buckshot had been the traditional way to go. We were definitely outside the norm, and I was the ringleader of this renegade sect. To think one could take a whitetail consistently past forty yards was unthinkable. They would all have stroked had they known what I was taking with my trusty 30–06! We had a liberal "buck a day" bag limit plus some "doe days" scattered through the winter months, and success was not difficult to achieve if simply taking a deer was your end point. Still, I was frustrated, rarely taking a buck with more than four points, and just didn't feel like I knew what the deer were doing. The truth is, I didn't. Sometimes it seemed the soybean fields would be full of deer and then other times, nothing. I could see no real pattern to their movement or their feeding habits. To move into the woods on their terms with a bow seemed utterly hopeless.

Bow Hunting Schools

Then, I met a real whitetail hunter, Ronnie Groom, a sporting goods retailer from Panama City, Florida. I was helping with some outdoor skills schools at Westervelt Lodge (www.WesterveltLodge.com) in West Alabama, and Fred Bear was sponsoring a bow hunting school at the lodge. Ronnie, Fred, and a delightful gent from Pensacola, Florida, named Hugh Blackburn, were the instructors. In spite of Fred Bear's fame, Ronnie was clearly the man with the plan. Fred had reached the pinnacle of his notoriety by this time, having bow hunted big game worldwide. Fred did not climb trees, but man could he shoot a recurve! Hugh, on the other hand, was a national champion target archer and was helping launch Bear's first series of compound bows. Remember the Delta V™ and the Brown Bear™? I was helping keep the squirrel population on the 14,000-acre lodge expanse in check with a sweet custom Cochise thumbhole equipped Anchuz 54 .22 Sporter and couldn't imagine trying to take a whitetail with a bow. After lunch one day, Ronnie pulled me off from the crowd and said, "Bob, why don't you join us? You already know more than most folks about hunting whitetails, and I can teach you to shoot a bow. You'll love it." Well, he was right. I did love it. Fred Bear provided bows and all the Razorheads™ we could shoot, and before long I could hit a pickup truck from ten yards pretty consistently!

Ronnie Groom and Bob Sheppard. Bow Hunting School 1979

Armed with what seemed at the time a ridiculous handicap, we were off to the woods. I had already concluded that sitting in a tree waiting on a whitetail to wonder within range of my 30–06 seemed completely fruitless. How in the world Ronnie thought we could get close enough to kill one of these wary animals with a bow was laughable. At that point, in Alabama, one could take a buck and a doe per day with a bow. In spite of how incredibly liberal this bag limit seemed, most of us thought the deer had little to worry about. I was wrong. That afternoon, Ronnie came to pick me up, and on the tailgate of his truck laid a heavy beamed six-point and a doe! Both had clean Bear™ Razorheads™ punched through both lungs. To say the least, I was impressed. After supper, I cornered Ronnie and said, "You gotta teach me how to do that." Ronnie is a quiet, unassuming sort of guy, a delight to be around, and an astute teacher and hunter. He had already taken hundreds of whitetails at that point in his career and was well known in his hometown to be the finest hunter around. I've met a lot of really accomplished hunters in the last thirty years, but few could conceptualize what they know and even fewer could teach it to others. Ronnie was one of those rare folks who could do both. Most consistently successful hunters can go into the woods and find a good ambush point for whitetails, but few can stand at that location and tell you exactly why it is a good place. Ronnie's expertise, as I would learn, went far beyond these basics.

For the next twenty years, I watched his every move, questioned every aspect of his techniques, and slowly, ever so slowly, began to see the patterns. Looking back, I don't understand why it was so hard to grasp, but I'll admit, that it was.

By the mid-1980s, Ronnie and I had taken our dog and pony show on the road to commercial hunting lodges across much of the South. As I began to grasp the concepts, I started to develop computer-based graphics presentations to illustrate the components of our hunting techniques. The more effective our teaching techniques became, the popularity of our hunting schools exploded. We enjoyed exposure to some of the finest whitetail hunting the world had to offer. These were the days before the Outdoor Channel™, before hunting videos and before the internet. With more exposure to better hunting, both our understanding of the basics were further refined.

Now looking back, I can see that we were blessed to see America's whitetail hunting at its peak. We hunted wild animals on huge expanses of timbered land with no fences, no feeding, no dogs, and no special breeding, yet took dozens of magnificent trophies.

By the late 1980s, we had forged relationships with the best of the commercial whitetail hunting operations in the country, and my skill with a computer was beginning to pay off. I had written an electronic medical records software package (EMR) in 1985 and by the following year had begun to add other physicians in the county where I practiced to it. This work with a relational database allowed me to begin working with statistical analysis. One afternoon sitting in a tree at Bent Creek Lodge (www.BentCreekLodge.com) in about 1987, I had a bang of an idea. I would write a computer database program that would allow the lodge to manage the details of their hunting operation, and we would tie this database into the NOAA (National Oceanic & Atmospheric Administration) database of weather elements. Herein lay the opportunity to take advantage of thousands of hunter days of experience without my having to do all the work. That night after supper I talked over the idea with the lodge owners, Johnny Lanier and Leo Allen, and they agreed with the concept. It took me the better part of the following year to pull it off, but by the fall season of 1988, I had it ready. Every morning and every afternoon, the lodge would send about twenty-five hunters into the woods to hunt on the massive 45,000-acre expanse of the lodge's land holdings. Each day at lunch, we would pull down the NOAA weather variables ... temperature, barometric pressure, wind direction, wind velocity, moonrise time, moonset time, moon phase, cloud cover conditions, precipitation, and integrate these data into our hunting database. Bear in mind, this was before the World Wide Web was in existence. When the hunters returned to the lodge for lunch, the lodge guides would accumulate data on what they had seen as well as what they killed, and this data was then linked to the weather information from the NOAA database. The same was the case each afternoon. Most commercial hunting operations in the South tend to place their hunters in the woods in the morning and on fields in the afternoon. Armed with the data from this very analytical approach, I could begin to unravel which variables really had an impact on whether we saw deer, but also even why we saw them. Because we have captured both sighting and kill data, we could even determine statistical data on kills by age class. For example, what are the statistical odds of taking a buck in the three and a half-year age class under a given set of conditions?

Computerized Deer Hunting

Boy, did I get an education. Obviously, with years of hunting success and experience, I had a lot of preconceived ideas about when deer would get up and walk around in the daytime and even thought I knew why (under what conditions) they might do so, at least some of the time. After compiling the first two years of data, I began to analyze it. The moon has fascinated hunters for centuries, and there is much published about the lunar effect on the earth's animals. I was eager to see what the data confirmed with respect to the whitetail. For example, based upon my hunting experience, I would have thought that hunting success during the day following a night of bright moon phase would not be as good. In other words, if the deer had good light through the night, they would be up feeding all night, and hence hunting the following day would not be as good. Indeed, when I looked at the numbers under varying conditions, the days following dark moon phases were clearly better with nearly a fourfold increase in the likelihood of success on days following dark moon phases. The data confirmed my experience. In years to follow I started to look more specifically at moonrise times and other variables such as cloud cover, precipitation, wind velocity, barometric pressure, and temperature. Then suddenly, a fly appeared in the ointment. During the fourth and fifth years of data collection, the effect of nighttime moon phase on the statistical odds of seeing and/or taking a deer reversed! In other words, the best hunting days during those seasons were the days following the nights of bright moon phase. I was stumped. By this time we had accumulated more than five thousand hunter days (the equivalent of you or me going hunting five thousand times, writing down what we saw and/or killed each time we went, and then matching this to the daily weather patterns). This allowed us to move from univariate to multivariate statistical analytical methods. If you have a data set with only a few hundred pieces of data, you really only have enough statistical power to analyze a single variable like, say, wind direction. However, you have no way of knowing for certain whether the variable you are focused upon is having a cause and effect relationship upon the variable

you are studying or just happens to be a marker for that effect

Analogy from Medicine

Let me explain using a completely different type of data. For more than a hundred years physicians have known that people who had what we call ventricular ectopy (the heart skipping beats in a particular way that we call premature ventricular complexes, or PVCs) had the tendency to experience sudden death more frequently than folks who do not have this type ectopy. The logical conclusion we all drew was that the PVCs lead to ventricular tachycardia (a lethal rapid type of heart rhythm) and sudden cardiac death. Hence any time we found a person with a lot of these PVCs we jumped on them with everything but the kitchen sink. We had a variety of medications in our armament that had been shown to reduce the frequency of these abnormal beats in the heart's rhythm. We would start the person on one of these medications and gradually increase the dosing until all, or nearly all, the PVCs disappeared. In the mid-1980s a drug came along that, for the first time, was really effective at making PVCs go away. It was called Flecainide™. The bulk of my practice of medicine was in the subspecialty of cardiology, and therefore I had a lot of patients on this medication. There had been dozens of studies looking at these drugs' effectiveness at making PVCs go away and this one was clearly the all time winner. Cardiologists across the country were using it like salt and pepper. Then the NIH (National Institute of Health) funded a study looking at a huge number of patients on this and other drugs. The study was focused not just on one variable (the PVCs) but also on others, like the sudden death rate as well as all cause mortality. In other words, they had enough patients in the study to look not just at the effect of the drug's ability to make PVCs go away, but also to look at other variables, like the sudden death rate among the patients taking a variety of doses and drugs. Sure enough, Flecainide's ability to make the PVCs go away was sterling. However, about eighteen months into the study, the NIH, one Friday afternoon, suddenly issued an emergent bulletin to physicians across the country indicating that the sudden death rate in the group of patients taking Flecainide was nearly three times as high as those in the placebo arm of the trial! So, it turns out that PVCs can be a marker for sudden death, but clearly not necessarily the cause of sudden death in most cases.

Flecainide™ is still on the market today, and should you be taking it, don't get your drawers in a wad and stop taking it because of what I have said here! It has been shown to be very effective in other types of heart arrhythmias while not causing an increase in the death rate.

Howling at the Moon

As you can see, having a data set large enough to utilize a multivariate approach to data analysis can keep you from drawing some very wrong conclusions. Now, to go back to our example of the moon phase, I had drawn the conclusion based upon my hunting experience, that when the moon phase was bright at night, the effect on hunting the following day was bad. In other words, I drew a cause and effect conclusion based upon my observations of a data set that was both too small (only a few hundred hunting trips) and univariate (looking at only one variable without knowing what effect other variables might be simultaneously having). By the beginning of the fifth year of data collection, we had more than five thousand hunting trips to analyze. In addition, we had collected data not just on the one variable (the moon phase), but also the moonrise time, moonset time, wind direction, wind velocity, barometric pressure, temperature, temperature change, cloud cover, precipitation, etc. We had enough data to hold certain variables within a set range while simultaneously checking for the true cause and effect another variable might have on our outcome (the odds of seeing and/or taking a whitetail in the daytime). It turned out that purely by chance, the days following the bright moon phases of those first two seasons were relatively warm. The days following the bright moon phases of the third and fourth seasons were relatively cold. Hence, it turned out to be the temperature that was driving deer sightings rather than the moon phase. In subsequent seasons, I've seen years when the data were mixed. In other words, some days following bright moon phases were warm while others were cold. Every time we look at the variables across large subsets of data using the multivariate approach, it is the temperature that seems to have a cause and effect relationship upon deer sightings/kills, not the moon phase! Let me say this another way to make it more clear. If I look at the data from hunting trips on days following nights with a bright moon phase, but warm weather, the sighting/kill results are dismal. However, if I look at hunting trips on days following nights with a bright moon phase, but cold weather, the results are stunningly good. That's what I mean by a true cause and effect relationship.

Hunters, by our very nature, are observers. We go to the woods, see deer activity, observe what time of day it occurred, notice how cold it was, how windy it was, etc., and based upon those observations involving multiple factors, draw certain conclusions. The problem is that just like with our computer based data observation, we sometimes are looking at the right variables, but still drawing the wrong conclusions. Let me illustrate with another example.

Timing the Rut

As hunters, we go into the woods each season, see bucks chasing does, and conclude, "The rut has begun!" We notice that it is December 19. We conclude the rut started this year on December 19. The following year we don't see any "rutting activity" until January 3. We are seeing the right variables, but from observing them, draw the wrong conclusions.

Biologists know that if you go to a given region of the country and sample a group of does from the herd in April, you find that by backdating the fetal ages from these deer, the rut

31

occurs between certain dates pretty consistently for that region year after year. In west central Alabama where I hunt, it is typically December 20 to December 30. In Kansas where I hunt with a friend, it is November 2 to November 12. In south Florida, it may be mid-September. Why is it then, that we noticed the rutting activity across a wide range of dates from year to year? Well, there are at least two variables at work here. First, bucks are bucks! If there is only one doe in the herd that has entered her estrus cycle, he will chase anything with four legs that resembles a doe. So you may see a buck chasing a doe at most any time of the season. However, the bulk of the does come into their estrus cycle during a fairly narrow date range based upon the individual deer's age and the genetics that triggers that estrus. For example, in the area of west central Alabama near my home, the peak of the rut falls between December 20 and December 30 each year. However, there is a light flurry of rutting activity shortly after Thanksgiving and another flurry in late January each year. What is causing this? A doe that is four and a half years old in this area will likely enter her first estrus cycle for a given year early in the winter (around Thanksgiving). There won't likely be many four and a half-year-old does in a naturally occurring herd, and hence, there won't be much activity spurred on at this time. The two and a half and three and a half-year-old does in the herd and a portion of the one and a half-year-old does (the bulk of the herd) will enter their estrus around Christmas, hence the "peak of the rut" for our area. The balance of the does in the herd, about one fourth to one-half of the one and a half-year-old does will not enter their first estrus until late January. This triggers a light rutting flurry toward the end of our hunting season.

But this is still not the whole picture. What if, for a given season, you take off work and hunt every day from December 20 to December 30, but the weather is rainy and unseasonably warm? That's right; you see very little evidence of the rut because the weather has the bulk of the herd's daytime movement activity pushed into nighttime hours. However, if you wait until April, and sample two dozen does from your herd, you find that nearly every one of them will have been fertilized between those same dates, December 20 to December 30! As a hunter, you just saw little if any evidence of the rut because the deer herd was nearly completely nocturnal. Now, the following season, you give it one last try, take off those few days from work, and hunt every day. On December 23, it rains you out all day. By dark the wind is howling from the southwest. Through the night, the temperature drops thirty degrees, and the next morning, it is bright, clear, cold as a witch, and you stumble from your vehicle only

33

to see an eight-point running down the road chasing a doe toward you. You rush to your tree stand, climb, and have a spike chase a doe under you while you are climbing. By the time it gets light enough to see, you can hear deer running in the thicket behind you. At 9:15 a.m., a two hundred-pound bruiser runs out of the bushes twenty yards to your left, and you place a three-blade broadhead neatly between his ribs. You are so excited you can barely contain yourself. You load him up, drive back to the camp house, and spend the next week retelling the tale of how the rut has exploded into action on Christmas Eve this year. Well, you are drawing the right conclusion, but for the wrong reason. As with the example above, sampling does in April again reveals they were nearly all bred during that same date range from December 20 to December 30. The cold weather had not a thing to do with the timing of the rut. You, as a hunter and observer, simply had it brought to your attention because the same deer herd that had been nocturnal the prior year because of the warm weather was pushed into more daytime activity by the sudden drop in the temperature on December 23 or 24. For a given geographic region, the bulk of the does in the herd are fertilized during approximately the same period from year to year. Some years it may be clear that the rut is occurring, but during others the woods may be pretty silent in the daylight. It is the genetics of the whitetail that is the variable driving the timing of the rut, not the temperature. Other variables can be at play without our realizing it. We tend to see the most obvious variables, not necessarily the one that is having the cause and effect relationship.

Eighty miles to the south of where I live, the peak of the rut falls between January 15 and January 25. A hundred miles to the north, near the Bankhead National Forest, the rut peaks in November. This is driven in a given localized herd primarily by genetics with the age structure of the particular herd playing a smaller part in the timing as noted above. The weather has little to do with when the does are actually fertilized.

So, you can see that it's not really difficult for us to draw some really wrong conclusions from what we observe in the woods as hunters. Having a very large (more than 35,000 hunter days!) and structured database allows us to look under the hood with some extra wrenches in our tool set, and draw conclusions no single hunter could ever visualize accurately, except by chance. What I will do in this book is temper a vast amount of successful hunting experience with data analysis from a gargantuan structured hunting database. I've taken more than a thousand whitetails, including several hundred with a bow. I don't mean to boast, but I think it is important for the reader to understand that exceedingly few hunters in world history have had this kind of exposure to the whitetail. I suspect that when my generation is gone, this tradition and knowledge will fade from American culture as we plunge headlong into European-style socialism. Certainly no rational person would argue that we have far more whitetails now than the Native Americans enjoyed. We have far better equipment, climbing tree stands, insect repellent, excellent weather predictions, and the ability to alter habitat to optimize hunting. As a private practicing physician, I had the control over my time to maximize my hunting efforts over several decades. I had access to thousands of acres of prime whitetail habitat. I have been fortunate to live in a state with a huge deer herd (more than two million) and very liberal bag limits (two deer per day for a one hundred plus day long season!). All these things bring to focus a very unusual opportunity. I know these numbers seem unthinkable to some hunters, and for this I sincerely apologize. I'll admit I'm not a purist hunter. I hunt because I love to hunt. I love the challenge. I love the animals. I love to shoot. I love the habitat. And I love venison. I love sharing that experience with others. Just to qualify and remain on our state's whitetail management system for much of the last twenty years, I must take thirty or so deer from our lease each year. So, as you can see, a lot of factors came to bear, almost like a perfect storm of elements that set the stage for my story of hunting success.

Getting Some Experience

That reminds me of a bow hunting school Ronnie Groom and I were doing years ago. After lunch the first day standing outside in the cool autumn breeze, we were going over some general hunting concepts with the group of hunters, and I was explaining that I felt each of the guests should probably not try to be trophy hunters right out of the chute. Even after taking hundreds of whitetails with a bow, dozens of wonderful trophies, I still take the first legal deer that shows up. To me, bow hunting is a fun sport, not a purist's pursuit. Now for certain, if a mature buck is the first to show, he gets the medicine! During the first afternoon of the bow school at Bent Creek Lodge last fall, the first deer by me was a tall three and a half-year-old eight-point. As he approached my position, I eased my bow to full draw, settled the single pin on his chest, and slowly pressed the release. He bounced about twelve yards, stopped in some thick cane near a creek to look back, and a few seconds later fell over still in plain view of my perch in a sweet gum. Ten minutes later, a mature doe shows up, and you guessed it. She got a three blade Wasp™ as well. She made it almost twenty-five yards before piling up. At any rate, following my own advice, I recommended that each try to take a dozen or so does with his/her bow before holding out for a trophy buck. In doing so, one could dramatically improve the odds of pulling off a successful shot when that magic moment finally arrived.

Finally, a gentleman from a Midwestern state looked at Ronnie and said, "I don't understand. In my home state, we can only take one tagged deer per season. If I use my tag on a doe, my season is over. What would you do in that situation?"

Ronnie looked intently at the fellow, glanced at me then said without further hesitation, "I'd move!" So, yes, Ronnie and I have been blessed to enjoy some of the finest whitetail hunting the world has ever seen. For that, we make no apologies. We wish all of you could have been with us for the ride.

Basic Hunting Strategies

Obviously, from what I've said already, my hunting strategies have evolved over a lifetime of hunting. In the early days, my success came from glassing large soybean fields. As I ventured into bow hunting, I favored food plots hosting a variety of grains like wheat, rye, oats, and in more recent years, a host of other plants including clover and other legumes. I slowly learned about naturally occurring food sources, like American beauty berries, swamp chestnut white oak acorns, overcup acorns, persimmons, wild grapes, and others. But as my experience matured, I slowly drifted away from fields of any kind, moving deeper into wooded forests using the whitetail's basic movement patterns to choose an ambush site. In later years, I would come to avoid food sources of any kind, preferring instead to hunt close to where the whitetail spends his daytime hours. More on this later.

In spite of my lengthy experience with this subject matter, I must admit that I struggle with just where to start here. In our bow schools, I utilize a series of slide presentations and computer graphics to illustrate my basic hunting strategy, but writing it down presents more of a challenge.

In an attempt to state the obvious, most of us think of a spot in the woods or a spot near the edge of a field or food plot as a "stand site," in other words, a place where we would hunt under certain conditions. My hunting is no different. But how we choose these potential spots and how we approach them form the key components to successful whitetail hunting. As I mentioned earlier about my Yankee friend from Ohio, walking into thousands of acres of wooded timberland to find one of these sweet spots can be intimidating. If you hunt the Midwest where the only trees grow along creeks and ditches between expanses of fields, or in Ohio where much of the timbered land is in small "woodlots" comprising only a few acres, all this fuss about where to hunt can seem a bit arcane. But again, that's not my history. These large expanses of timbered woodland are more akin to what our Native Americans had to deal with and present a tough challenge to even the most sage whitetail enthusiast.

The Inexperienced Hunter

Imagine a completely inexperienced hunter walking off into a large expanse of timber in search of a spot to hunt. He likely parked his vehicle close to the edge of the timber, perhaps near a road. He did so with little foreknowledge of where he planned to end up hunting. As he walks into the woods, he has no clue from which direction the wind is blowing. He has little idea of what a good spot might look like should he stumble upon one. He certainly has no idea of where the deer might be going should one decide to get up and walk around, and he has no idea of whether the weather conditions he's immersed in are ideal for effectively hunting a whitetail. His odds of taking a whitetail are quite dismal.

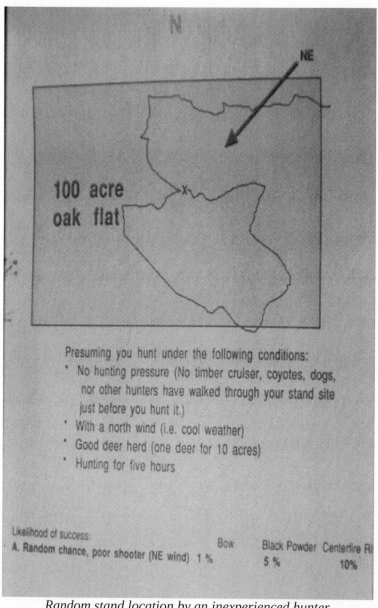

Presuming you hunt under the following conditions:
* No hunting pressure (No timber cruiser, coyotes, dogs, nor other hunters have walked through your stand site just before you hunt it.)
* With a north wind (i.e. cool weather)
* Good deer herd (one deer for 10 acres)
* Hunting for five hours

Likelihood of success:

	Bow	Black Powder	Centerfire Ri
A. Random chance, poor shooter (NE wind)	1 %	5 %	10%

Random stand location by an inexperienced hunter

Even if we assume ideal conditions...habitat with a good herd density (about a deer for ten to twenty acres), cool weather, hence likely a north wind, little hunting pressure, and of course, hunting for several hours, our inexperienced hunter has less than a 1 percent chance of taking a deer with a bow, and maybe 5 to 10 percent with a centerfire rifle. How do those odds stack up against your own experience? Be honest with yourself. Would you be able to take a whitetail one out of every ten times you went hunting? That is exactly how I felt when I started. Well, let me encourage you. As I have proven dozens of times in our bow schools over the last thirty years, given this set of pretty good conditions, I can come very close to a 100 percent odds of returning to the lodge with a deer I've taken with a bow ...every day! And so can you. But the devil is in the details. The problem is which details are really important to a successful hunter? Using scents effectively? Wearing the right camo pattern? Using a seventy-pound high performance bow with five pins? Choosing the right grunt call? Climbing to thirty feet? Employing a good set of rattling antlers? Using thirty-dollar high-quality mechanical broadheads? The answer is an emphatic, "No!" Although there may be a place for the occasional use of these techniques, I place little value on any of these factors to ensure my success. I shoot a simple fifty pound bow stripped of most of the market gimmicks...a rest and single pin, a high quality release, and a peep. That's it. In the years I hunted with a recurve, the setup was even more simplistic ...a single pin and tab release. I rarely climb more than fifteen feet. I never use scents, calls, nor rattling antlers to get deer within bow range. I wear simple, comfortable clothing (sometimes camo, sometimes not...makes zero difference to me), no face mask, no face paint, and no gloves (unless it's really cold). My broadheads are simple, cheap, three blade, fixed cutting leading edge Wasp™ heads. My arrows are light, carbon, and perfectly matched to my bow's weight and draw length. They are stabilized with simple four-inch, three-vane fletch, feathers when I shot a recurve. My hunting is simple, inexpensive, easy to apply, and requires few, if any, gimmicks. My wife, however, points out that you should benefit from the two million dollars it took for me to figure all this out!

My tree stand, I must confess, is homemade, but you can buy something similar from www.GuidosOutdoors.com, and I recommend that you do so.

The shooter can pivot 360 degrees around the tree.

Or the shooter can sit comfortably for hours.

I have treated far too many unfortunate hunters who fell from homemade stands to be comfortable with most home-constructed stands. I climb with simple screw in steps. I remain attached to the tree with a safety mechanism at two contact points going up, while I'm there, and coming down the tree. Safety is no place to be cutting corners. When I go to the woods, I am in no hurry, and my intention is that a whitetail is coming home with me. I hold such confidence because I have been able to make it happen so many times in the past. You can do the same.

Back to our wandering hunter. What on earth is he looking for? He wanders about for a while, stumbles upon a nice tree where he can see in all directions, thinks this is it, and then second-guesses himself. He wanders around some more but realizes the day is slipping away then decides to return to the tree he favored earlier. Having ambled over some thirty acres with no knowledge of the wind direction, he has now scattered his scent over enough area to virtually ensure that no deer will come within bow range for the rest of the day. No surprise at what he sees ...five squirrels, a possum, a woodpecker, and two cold biscuits, sans sausage. Coffee was good though.

A Choice Spot

There was likely nothing particularly bad about our hunter's choice of a spot to hunt. It just needed a few important features added to make it, well, more ideal. What features? Let's start with where he parked his vehicle. How often do we drive to the same place in spite of where we're going to hunt? Big mistake. If he had for example, a northeast wind (a wind blowing from the northeast toward the southwest), he should have parked his vehicle on the southwest side of the hundred-acre woodlot he planned to hunt. From there, instead of wandering around, he should have done his scouting to locate this spot the previous year after the deer season, perhaps during turkey season in the early spring. He then would have known where he was going before he started. He could use a compass (or, these days, perhaps a GPS) to walk directly to the spot, walking always into the wind on his way to the spot he plans to hunt. Just by walking to his spot facing into the wind, he has significantly increased his odds of success (from 1 percent to 5 percent—a five-fold improvement!). Five percent odds of success is still pitiful, but he's now moving in the right direction. Stick with me. I will begin to make sense as we put the pieces of this vexing hunting puzzle together.

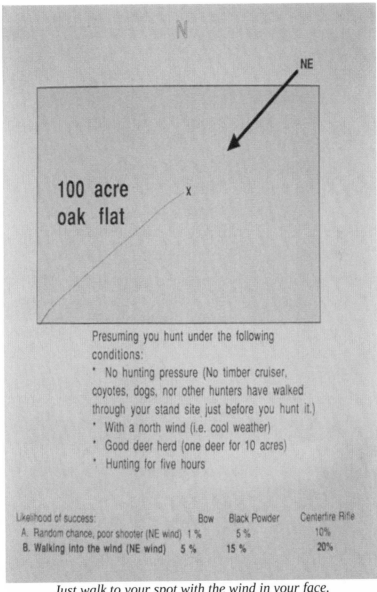

Presuming you hunt under the following conditions:

* No hunting pressure (No timber cruiser, coyotes, dogs, nor other hunters have walked through your stand site just before you hunt it.)
* With a north wind (i.e. cool weather)
* Good deer herd (one deer for 10 acres)
* Hunting for five hours

Likelihood of success:	Bow	Black Powder	Centerfire Rifle
A. Random chance, poor shooter (NE wind)	1 %	5 %	10%
B. Walking into the wind (NE wind)	5 %	15 %	20%

Just walk to your spot with the wind in your face.

So far, we have a backdrop of an open hardwood forest and a hunter that has, for the most part, simply wandered into the woods (granted, now walking facing the wind) to about the middle of the woodlot. Think about what it might have done to our hunter's odds of success if there had been a body of water, in this case, a slough, projecting into the woodlot from the southeast? Now, our hunter is hunting on a "point." Although it may not seem like much of an important feature, look at what hunting on a point does to the statistical likelihood of a deer wandering by you. Now the hunter's odds have increased another three fold ...to about 15 percent.

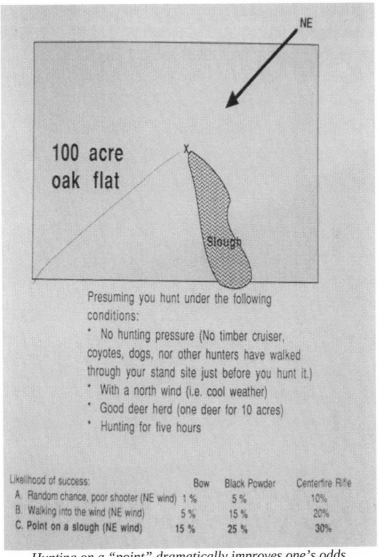

NE

100 acre oak flat

Slough

Presuming you hunt under the following conditions:
* No hunting pressure (No timber cruiser, coyotes, dogs, nor other hunters have walked through your stand site just before you hunt it.)
* With a north wind (i.e. cool weather)
* Good deer herd (one deer for 10 acres)
* Hunting for five hours

Likelihood of success:	Bow	Black Powder	Centerfire Rifle
A. Random chance, poor shooter (NE wind)	1 %	5 %	10%
B. Walking into the wind (NE wind)	5 %	15 %	20%
C. Point on a slough (NE wind)	15 %	25 %	30%

Hunting on a "point" dramatically improves one's odds.

Should you add a second point (in this case the corner of a field or pasture) that approaches the first point from the opposite direction, we again double our hunter's odds of success ...to around 30 percent. Be honest. If you could take a deer

with your bow one out of every three times you
go to the woods, wouldn't you be happy? Well,
you can. But we are not stopping here.
Remember, I said I could push the odds to better
than 90 percent.

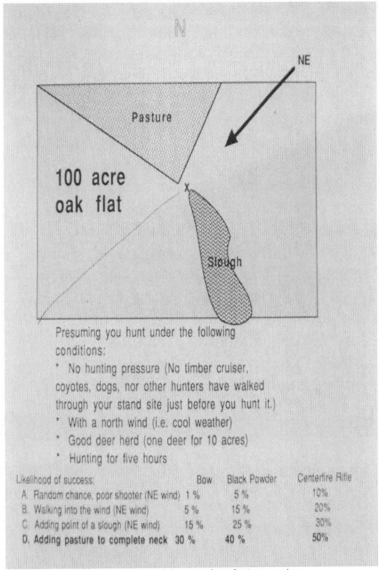

N

NE

Pasture

100 acre
oak flat

Slough

Presuming you hunt under the following
conditions:
* No hunting pressure (No timber cruiser,
coyotes, dogs, nor other hunters have walked
through your stand site just before you hunt it.)
* With a north wind (i.e. cool weather)
* Good deer herd (one deer for 10 acres)
* Hunting for five hours

Likelihood of success:	Bow	Black Powder	Centerfire Rifle
A. Random chance, poor shooter (NE wind) 1 %		5 %	10%
B. Walking into the wind (NE wind)	5 %	15 %	20%
C. Adding point of a slough (NE wind)	15 %	25 %	30%
D. Adding pasture to complete neck 30 %		40 %	50%

The hunter's odds are clearly improving.

With these two additional terrain features in
place, optimizing our "bottleneck" in the
woodlot, the need for a change in approach
comes to light. By walking into the northeast

wind from the southwest corner of the woodlot, we have walked through nearly half of the area from which we might expect a deer to have approached. We would be better served to walk up one side of the slough or the other, basically approaching the bottleneck from the southeast. But wait. That would have us no longer walking into the wind, right? Well, it becomes apparent that we should only hunt this spot when the wind is more ideal...from the northwest. With this approach, any deer feeding into the woods to the west of the bottleneck or from the east of the bottleneck will not have been spooked by our hunter's approach. In addition, while the hunter is sitting in his stand within the bottleneck, his scent is being constantly blown across the water behind him. Ideal, no? Look at our hunter's odds now...up another 10 percent to around 40 percent. We're not finished.

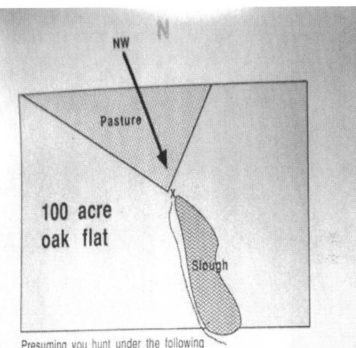

Presuming you hunt under the following conditions:
* No hunting pressure (No timber cruiser, coyotes, dogs, nor other hunters have walked through your stand site just before you hunt it.)
* With a north wind (i.e. cool weather)
* Good deer herd (one deer for 10 acres)
* Hunting for five hours

Likelihood of success:	Bow	Black Powder	Centerfire Rifle
A. Random chance, poor shooter (NE wind)	1 %	5 %	10%
B. Walking into the wind (NE wind)	5 %	15 %	20%
C. Adding point of a slough (NE wind)	15 %	25 %	30%
D. Adding pasturre to complete neck	30 %	40 %	50%
E. Hunt the neck on only a NW wind	40 %	60 %	60%

Our spot now demands a different wind direction to hunt effectively.

Food Source and Bedding Areas

What if we had a food source (food plot, cornfield, bean field, etc.) adjacent to the woodlot off to the southwest and a bedding area (clear cut, swamp, thicket, etc.) off to the northeast? If you were sitting in our bottleneck in the afternoon, from what direction might you expect the deer to approach? Well, how about from your right (northeast) moving to your left (southwest) ...walking from the bedding area (where the deer spend their daytime hours) from the northeast, toward the food source (where the deer tend to spend their night time hours feeding) off to the southwest? Adding these features to our setup adds another 15 percent...now 55 percent.

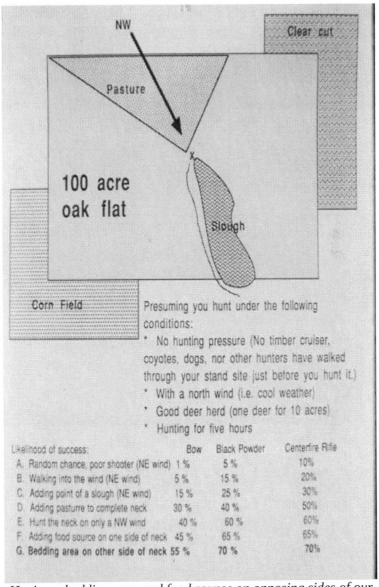

NW

Clear cut

Pasture

100 acre
oak flat

Slough

Corn Field

Presuming you hunt under the following conditions:
* No hunting pressure (No timber cruiser, coyotes, dogs, nor other hunters have walked through your stand site just before you hunt it.)
* With a north wind (i.e. cool weather)
* Good deer herd (one deer for 10 acres)
* Hunting for five hours

Likelihood of success:	Bow	Black Powder	Centerfire Rifle
A. Random chance, poor shooter (NE wind)	1 %	5 %	10%
B. Walking into the wind (NE wind)	5 %	15 %	20%
C. Adding point of a slough (NE wind)	15 %	25 %	30%
D. Adding pasture to complete neck	30 %	40 %	50%
E. Hunt the neck on only a NW wind	40 %	60 %	60%
F. Adding food source on one side of neck	45 %	65 %	65%
G. Bedding area on other side of neck	55 %	70 %	70%

Having a bedding area and food source on opposing sides of our spot improves the odds even more.

If you could take a whitetail with your bow every other time you went hunting, would you feel like a successful hunter? Well, again, you can. Think about what I've said so far. We have said we would hunt this spot (a bottleneck located within a 100-acre woodlot with a bedding area adjacent to it on one side and a food source adjoining it on the other side) when it is relatively cool, and a northwest wind is blowing, and that we would park our vehicle on the southeast corner of the woodlot and walk to the stand site up the side of the slough toward the northwest, with the wind in our face. I promise you, as long as you do that, you will be able to take a deer on average, every other time you go hunting. How many times in a season can you make this magic happen? Unfortunately only once! In other words, I would only hunt this outstanding place only once in a hunting season!

Not Over Hunting a Good Spot

Gee whiz, what a painful reality. First you paint me the picture of an ideal spot only to tell me I can only hunt it once per season! Well, you can hunt it all you want, but your odds of taking a deer there after that first trip, drop precipitously. The more times you hunt it, the closer to zero odds you will come. It goes something like this. The first time you hunt the spot (or any one else for that matter, so beware of your hunting buddies hunting your spot), your odds of success run about 50/50. The second time, you are down to about 15 percent. The third time, about 5 percent. After that, enjoy the squirrels! Discouraging, huh? Hunters are stunned at our schools when I say emphatically that I only hunt a spot once per season. I am constantly moving, very rarely bow hunting a spot more than once in a season. There can be exceptions with a rifle as we will discuss in more detail later, but even with a gun, I am picky about where I will hunt. The conditions must be near perfect and the spot pristine for the season at hand. Rarely will I frequent a spot regardless of what I take on the first hunt of the season. In fact, I anticipate that if I take a deer in a particular spot, that will be the only deer I take from that spot until the following season.

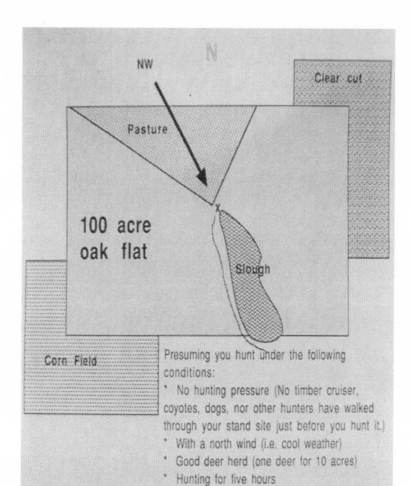

Presuming you hunt under the following conditions:
* No hunting pressure (No timber cruiser, coyotes, dogs, nor other hunters have walked through your stand site just before you hunt it.)
* With a north wind (i.e. cool weather)
* Good deer herd (one deer for 10 acres)
* Hunting for five hours

Likelihood of success:	Bow	Black Powder	Centerfire Rifle
A. Random chance, poor shooter (NE wind)	1 %	5 %	10%
B. Walking into the wind (NE wind)	5 %	15 %	20%
C. Adding point of a slough (NE wind)	15 %	25 %	30%
D. Adding pasturre to complete neck	30 %	40 %	50%
E. Hunt the neck on only a NW wind	40 %	60 %	60%
F. Adding food source on one side of neck	45 %	65 %	65%
G. Bedding area on other side of neck	55 %	70 %	70%
H. Adding ability to shoot well	70 %	80 %	85%
I. Hunting the stand infrequently	75 %	85 %	90%
J. When and how to take the shot	85 %	90 %	95%

The odds now reflect a skilled hunter never over hunting a spot.
I cannot say enough about this to drive the point home, but let me dig the hole a little deeper. Going in to a spot you plan to hunt to put up a tree stand in advance, to work on a tree stand in advance, to video what might be frequenting the area, having a hunting buddy hunt a spot at some point in the season before you hunt it, hunt ing the spot with the wrong wind direction...These activities will absolutely destroy your odds of success, even if you are otherwise hunting the spot under ideal conditions with a perfect approach into the wind.

I am so fanatic about this, that when my personal hunting club was organized, here's what I told my members."Okay, guys, this club is not a democracy. What we have here is a benevolent dictatorship. The leases are in my name. I will be fair, but I make the rules. We have about six thousand acres between the six of us. We'll work the roads, plant the fields, and do all the club work in the spring and late summer together. But we break up the club into approximate one thousand-acre tracts. Each of us takes a tract, and once the fields are planted, no one enters any other hunter's tract. Period. If I catch you on my tract, you'll be looking for another club to join. Any questions?"

Howls of protest went up immediately. They knew my reputation and quickly retorted,"We know what you will do! You know the land where the best spots are, and you'll pick the best area, and we will be stuck with what's left."

To which I responded,"I suspected that's what you would say, so here's the deal. Each of you get together and decide who gets which tract of land. When each of you has chosen a tract, I will take whatever is left." They all just stood there, mouths aghast, dumbfounded at my response. Little did they realize just how seriously I take this hunting pressure issue. The best of spots is worthless when it's been hunted to death. Although to keep peace in the club, I've had to swap tracts several times in the last fifteen years. In spite of some persisting doubt, my kill statistics demand that I am right.

What Is Hunting Pressure, Anyway?

I should digress at this point to explain why I am so dogmatic about this aspect of my hunting tactics. When we use the term "hunting pressure," most of us really don't understand just what this entails. Deer are not logical, analytical creatures. They do not lie off somewhere in a thicket thinking, Let's see now, Sheppard parked his truck on the southeast side of this thicket this morning. That must mean he's going to circle around to the west side of the ditch and try to ambush us at the north end of the slough. Deer have no such ability to think abstractly. That does not mean they are stupid. But how is it that they can tell where we will be and avoid that area so consistently? Well, first, we must remember the obvious. Deer are primarily nocturnal animals. But what does this mean? Do they cease to exist when it gets daylight? Not so. All night long, they wander about at complete peace. They walk the roads, come into your backyard, browse the fields and woodlots, and generally cover much of the terrain they dominate according to their herd's pecking order. When daylight begins to approach, more than 90 percent of the herd returns to the "bedding area" where they spend the bulk of the daytime hours. A bedding area means a place with features that you as a human will not penetrate. It usually means a thicket, swamp, clear cut, or some other piece of ground with so many briars, brambles, bushes, stumps, logs, and other obstruction that you would have to crawl to get through it, and even then, it would be difficult. That is where the deer are located when it is daylight. They usually don't venture out of these "sanctuaries" until well after dark, and they are back at home here well before daylight the following morning. So, as hunters, the odds are stacked against us from the start. On a warm day with little if any wind, less than one percent of the herd in a given area will leave the confines of these bedding areas in the light of day. Under more ideal conditions, say for example, cool breezy weather, as many as one in ten of these deer might get up and venture into an open woodlot during daylight hours. But anyway you cut it, we are hunting odds that are stacked against us by a predominantly nocturnal animal. Don't forget that. Do so, and you will spend an inordinate amount of time enjoying the squirrels. Let me put it this way. When the hunting season comes in, I watch the weather. If the weather is not ideal, I fish, work, write, or finish my honey-dos. I pick the best places in my tract to hunt, and I don't enter the woods until the conditions are near perfect. That can be most frustrating at times, but I've learned the hard way, never violate this principle unless you really like those squirrels. I can hear the howls of protest, saying, "But I can't take off work just any time I want. I have to go hunting when I'm off." Like I said elsewhere in this book, my success is a result of diligence, patience, timing, good hunting area, becoming a skilled hunter, a job that allows me complete control of my schedule, and about three percent dumb luck.

Back to the "hunting pressure" issue. How is it that deer actually pattern hunters? After all, aren't we supposed to be patterning them? Think about this. One crisp morning, you walk into a woodlot, locate a favored spot, attach your stand to a tree, lay your pack on the ground, kneel to assemble your gear, climb with your hands all over the tree, and attach your safety belt while hugging the tree. Get the picture? You are all over the spot. Your scent is attached to millions of particles of bark, leaves, grass, bushes, and debris. By the end of a morning's hunt, you have not only saturated a segment of the area with your scent where you walked in and out, but also left your scent concentrated all around the tree you climbed. It is primarily this part of your scent that is physically attached to the environment that gives you away. That night, deer will wander through this area and smell where you have been. Much like a dog that can track a person days later from the scant scent left on a piece of his clothing, these astute animals know human smell (danger!) when they sense it. They don't run off into a thicket. They are perfectly comfortable during the nighttime hours. But that scent burns the presence of danger into their simple, but very effective little minds, and they simply don't venture into this area again during daylight. They will feed there every night at will. Tracks, scrapes, and rubs will abound. But it's all done under the cover of night. Sure, there are exceptions. We've all seen them. But hunt the exceptions ...and enjoy the squirrels. Enough said. Did I say, "Don't over hunt your good spots"?

Now, let's continue to refine the characteristics of an ideal spot. So far, we have a place located within a hundred-acre woodlot, a bedding area on one side and food source on the other side. We have two terrain features (the point of a slough, corner of a pasture, point on a creek, point of a ridge, etc.) creating a "bottleneck." We approach this spot from the south, walk to it with the wind in our face, and set up on the south edge of the bottleneck facing north. This allows the deer movement pattern between the bedding area and food source to pass naturally along an east/west path (east to west in the afternoon and west to east in the morning) upwind of the hunter. With this common feeding pattern in mind, take a look at what happens when the bottleneck is located nearer to the bedding area.

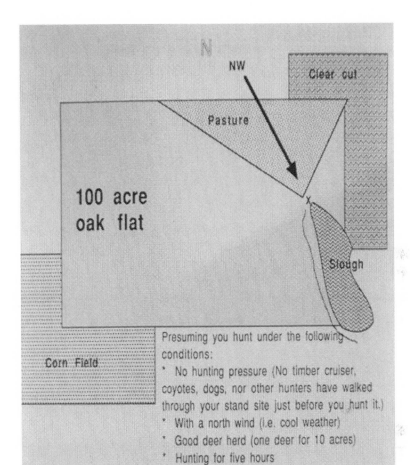

Presuming you hunt under the following conditions:

* No hunting pressure (No timber cruiser, coyotes, dogs, nor other hunters have walked through your stand site just before you hunt it.)
* With a north wind (i.e. cool weather)
* Good deer herd (one deer for 10 acres)
* Hunting for five hours

Likelihood of success:	Bow	Black Powder	Centerfire Rifle
A. Random chance, poor shooter (NE wind)	1 %	5 %	10%
B. Walking into the wind (NE wind)	5 %	15 %	20%
C. Adding point of a slough (NE wind)	15 %	25 %	30%
D. Adding pasturre to complete neck	30 %	40 %	50%
E. Hunt the neck on only a NW wind	40 %	60 %	60%
F. Adding food source on one side of neck	45 %	65 %	65%
G. Bedding area on other side of neck	55 %	70 %	70%
H. Adding ability to shoot well	70 %	80 %	85%
I. Hunting the stand infrequently	75 %	85 %	90%
J. When and how to take the shot	85 %	90 %	95%
K. Neck closer to the bedding area	90 %	95%	98%

We moved our bottleneck closer to the bedding area.

Think about this for a moment. We said that deer tend to leave the safety of the bedding area in the late evening hours moving toward the nighttime feeding area. It makes sense that if our ambush point is located very near the edge of their safety zone, then they are more likely to pass by us during legal hunting hours ...before dark. Our odds of taking a deer with a bow are now pushing the 90 percent range. With a rifle or black powder, it's just a matter of which one will you take, not whether you will take a deer.

How to Practice with a Bow

Now that we can recognize the characteristics of an ideal hunting spot when we see one, let us return to assessing the personal skills typical of a refined bow hunter.

Obviously, shooting practice is important, but most hunters agree that I have a pretty radical approach (more on that later). Before you can shoot well, your bow must be set up correctly. You can pick up a rifle off the shelf and after five minutes of sighting in, you can be ready to hunt (although most are not...more on this later as well). Purchasing a bow is more like buying a suit of clothes or a pair of shoes. If it doesn't fit, you will find it difficult to shoot well. The bow must have a draw weight that fits you. Whitetails are fairly small animals, and the lightest bows will punch through most of the time, even when a bone is encountered. So, in my opinion, you just don't need a heavy draw weight. The way I determine the ideal draw weight is to have the hunter point the bow directly at the target and very slowly draw it with no overarching, no use of shoulder and back muscles. Just point the bow at the deer and slowly ease it back. If you struggle the least bit, back the weight down a few pounds. I can easily pull seventy pounds, but I hunt with fifty pounds of draw weight. Once you have the ideal draw weight determined, draw length should be determined. There is not much room for error here. The ideal arrow length is determined by your arm length. You can fudge an inch or so, but more than this and you are asking for trouble with respect to consistent shot placement. The draw length is determined by measuring the distance from the nock on the string at full draw to about an inch past the arrow rest (to the back of the broadhead). With the draw length (and therefore arrow length) known, you can go to a chart (available in most any bow shop) and determine a reasonable guestimate of arrow spine (how stiff the arrow is). Different brands of arrows use a range of designations to determine spine. In other words, there is no standard nomenclature to determine arrow spine. In the years when we used aluminum arrows, this was not the case. The arrow's diameter and wall thickness were placed end to end to create a numerical value that served as a measure of arrow spine. For example a 1913 (which is what I shot) was a lighter spined arrow than a 2117 (21 hundredths of an inch in diameter and 17 thousandths of an inch tube wall thickness). All this makes little difference to the average hunter. Whatever setup you start with, just stick with it. Always buy the same brand and weight arrows; the same brand, style, and weight broadheads; and the same type and length of fletch. This allows you to maintain consistency, which is far more important that target accuracy.

With your arrows matched to your bow, the next thing to do is to make sure the combination will fly straight from your bow. All this is determined before you pay for the bow. If it won't fly straight, any reputable bow shop can help you check for other variables such as the positioning of your nock, cam adjustments, and making certain the arrow rest aligns the arrow so that it is centered in the draw plane both horizontally (left to right) and vertically (along the length of the bow, wheel to wheel). Sometimes the arrow spine will need to be adjusted up or down by one designation to get good arrow flight. Once all this is done (and I do it only once every five to ten years when I buy a new bow), you sight the bow in. That means shooting your bow at a target and adjusting the sight pin (and I recommend hunting with a single pin—more on this later) to hit the target, first with practice points, then with the broadhead you will hunt with. Again, all this is done pretty much one time when you buy the bow.

Take One Shot, Then Quit While You're Ahead

Once I have a new bow setup, this is where I depart from the traditional approach. I shoot a few arrows to make certain my arrow/ broadhead combination is flying true and hitting the target. I put my bow in its case and stop shooting! Each morning I take it out, climb to my practice platform, and shoot one arrow at each of three targets at varying distances. If I miss, I go inside. If I hit the kill zone dead center, I go inside. The next day, I go out sometime during the day and take one shot at each target. The third day, same sequence. If after a week or so, I'm consistently off target, then I check my setup again and make the necessary adjustments. But if I'm consistently hitting the kill zone at varying distances, I keep shooting only a single arrow each day at each target until the season arrives. By that point in time, I know with confidence that when the deer shows up, I can and will make the killing shot the first time I draw the bow, because that is the way I have practiced.

When you shoot and shoot and shoot during a practice session, you generally do one of two things. First, you start with a problem and then correct it by unconsciously changing the way you hold your bow. The next day, you start with the same mistake and then unconsciously correct it. This pattern will follow you to the woods. Second, if you start out hitting the target and keep shooting, you will fatigue and likely become less accurate with time, and this will rattle your confidence and you start to do dumb things trying consciously to correct the problem, like moving your sight pin, your rest, or worse, your peep. Either way, overzealous practice with a modern compound breeds bad shooting habits. Don't over do it. Practice the way you plan to kill deer ...one shot at a time. As you will see, this approach takes a great deal of self-discipline. There is a tremendous temptation to keep shooting. Just give it a try one season and see what it does to your confidence as the first deer approaches. The thought that I might miss never enters my mind! Every shot, short or long, is deliberate, calculated, and generally lethal.

How to Take the Shot

The next piece of personal skill to acquire is knowing when and how to take the shot. The best way to teach this skill is to have a hunter sit in the tree next to me and allow me to talk him through the deer's approach. I tell him when to move, when to remain still, when to draw, and when to take the shot. But some of this is common sense. Most hunters who sit with me in the woods are surprised to see that I am constantly moving ...at least until I spot a deer. At that instant, I am dead still, focused and immediately beginning to plan my shot. I try to see the deer when he is as far away from my stand as possible, hence my moving constantly to keep watch in all directions. Once I see the deer, I stand up and address his direction by placing my left shoulder toward him (I am a right-handed shooter, so the bow is in my left hand). That prepares me for the correct shooting position. I am confident shooting out to about fifty yards, so if that is as close as the deer is coming to me, I pick my moment and take the shot. If he is going to angle closer, then I will let him move into a more ideal position, but with every step he takes, I am recalculating where and when I will take the shot. If he suddenly looks the least bit spooked, I may take a shot at forty yards. But whatever the case, when he enters my thirty-yard circle, he's dead. I don't wait for a more ideal shot than this. When a deer gets that close, there are just too many things that can go wrong. I am certain I can take him within that thirty-yard circle, so I don't take any chances with something going wrong. Once he's inside that circle, I take the first lethal shot he presents. Again, I realize this is counter to general bow hunting wisdom, but I don't know of many people who have taken more whitetails than I have.

Look Him in the Eye

I would digress for a moment here. I have heard seemingly seasoned hunters say that it is not good to look a deer in the eye. Rather look past the deer or off in a slightly different direction. They seem to think the deer has a sixth sense and can just tell when he is being watched. This is pure nonsense! I stare them right in the eye from the moment they come into view. If they get close and even should look up at me, I just stare directly at them thinking all the while, It doesn't matter, sport. You are dead, and there is not a thing you can do about it! The key to executing those last thirty seconds, I am convinced, is to not think with your emotions. Think with your brain. When you draw, don't rush the shot...draw smooth, easy, and quietly. When you settle the pin on his side, steady it there for a few seconds before you release the arrow. Certainly, we all get excited when a deer gets into close quarters. But you must learn to control that excitement. You remain dead still until you are ready draw, and only then do you move. The only other time I move is when the deer is moving. If I need to change positions slightly, I wait until the deer is moving to make my move.

Cover is another setup feature where I depart from the norm. I

want absolutely no cover in or near the tree I'm perched in. I want the cover at the ground level where the deer is. I want nothing up at my eye level to block either my view or my ability to execute the shot in any direction. The ground level cover is to give the deer something to hide its eyes so you can get drawn to take the shot.

With these learned skills under our hunter's belt, the odds of taking a deer with a bow are approaching 85 percent! Not bad odds for a bowhunter, huh?

Feeding Patterns

Take another look at that last diagram. Notice that the bottleneck where we have been focusing our hunting efforts is closer to the bedding area and farther away from the food source. To understand what this means, think about what deer do in the woods day after day. They are on no schedule, no daylight savings time, no work schedule, no time clock, no set time to eat, no alarm clocks. By their nature, they are nocturnal, meaning when it gets dark, they get up and start to move around. Food is the primary driving force to their movements. The rut is a distant secondary reason they move around, but this is focused on just a few days during the season. Food is the key. Most of the good hunters I have known over the years know the deer's' primary food sources as the season progresses ...persimmons and American beautyberries early in the fall, then sawtooth, overcup, and a little later, mountain white oak and swamp chestnut acorns. Then come the various red oak acorns, food plots, and honeysuckle. Obviously these food sources vary across geographic regions, but the point is that for your hunting area, it is important to know what the deer might be feeding upon at a given time of the season. Having said that, I must confess that I virtually never hunt near food sources. Surprised? Well, you should not be. Never forget what I said earlier. Deer are nocturnal animals. That means most of the herd spends most of its daytime hours in a thicket where individual deer may get up, take a few steps, browse a little, then lay back down. They virtually never venture from this safe haven until the cover of night. The older the deer's age class, the more nocturnal he/she becomes. So, as you begin to form these concepts of what the deer are doing in your mind, remember this pattern. They spend the day in a thicket. As night approaches, individual deer, beginning with the youngest and least experienced in the herd, get up and start to wander toward the favored food source available at that particular time of the year. That means the overwhelming percentage of tracks you see were made at night...a time when you cannot hunt. So, don't hunt where you find a bunch of tracks. When the deer arrive, you will likely be at home eating supper. Through the nighttime hours, the entire deer herd leaves the safe haven of thickets and swamps and move out into open timber, fields, and roads seeking a variety of food sources. As morning approaches, the herd begins to move back toward the bedding area where they will spend the day. That cycle is played out year round. At any given moment, there may be somewhere between one percent and ten percent of the herd that is violating this law of nature. These few venture out of the bedding area during the daytime hours. It is this small percentage of the herd that we are hunting (although I have figured out a way to hunt them inside the bedding area—more on that later under "advanced hunting strategies").

The usual movement goes something like this. The youngest deer in the herd, typically young does and bucks are the first to leave the bedding area in late afternoon. With your bottleneck located near the bedding area (as opposed to positioning yourself at the food source), these young deer are the first ones you see in the afternoon (more on morning hunting later). The closer you can be to the bedding area, the higher the odds that something will venture by you during legal shooting hours. As you might guess, the older deer in the herd, older does and mature bucks, are the last to leave the safety of the bedding area in the evening. Positioning yourself in such a way to allow the younger deer to get by you, but without smelling you, is a skill only the most sage and experienced hunters master. Even with great skill, it is difficult to accomplish. When I'm bow hunting, this is why I take the first deer to arrive. I can most often do so before they get into a position to smell me and make a scene. The killing shot usually goes something like this. The deer are relaxed and in no hurry. They have slept through most of the day and are now slowly making their way toward the favored food source. When the first doe gets into position, I draw, settle the pin and release. The arrow punches through and sticks in the ground on the other side of the deer. The deer will bounce ten to fifteen yards and stop to look back at whatever caused the commotion. There seems to be no pain and more often than not, the deer will fall over standing in that same position. On a few occasions, I've seen the deer even go back to feeding and then fall over having no clue they were fatally wounded. The rest of the nearby deer usually trot off causing little disturbance and not having smelled the danger. Two hours later as dusk soaks up the light of day, the old bruiser materializes from the thicket. Often, he will see the dead doe, and this draws his attention. Perfect. His attention is elsewhere giving me the freedom to draw. As his chest clears a bush, I settle the pin, release, and the first scene is played out a second time. I make a point of continuing to hold my bow out in the shooting position following the shot. This does two important things. It helps me with good shooting form called follow through, and it keeps me still as the deer wheels to run, but stops to look back. My quiver is attached to the opposite side of the tree and my right hand starts to move in a very slow and calculated single motion to retrieve a second arrow. If the deer runs, I proceed with nocking a second arrow. If he stops to look back, I freeze. If he starts to walk, I proceed with the arrow retrieval. It is uncanny how frequently I've seen this scene unfold only to look around and see another deer approaching completely oblivious to the localized commotion. I've simply found that the act of taking a deer with a bow causes precious little disturbance in the whitetails' world. Knowing this is key to repeat success. Knowing that your odds of a second kill remain high in spite of what appeared to have been an awful commotion is important, because the exact same is true of a shot that missed its mark. Just nock another arrow and keep watching. If your setup and approach are good and the conditions are ideal, it's just a matter of time until another deer shows up.

An Afternoon to Remember

Allow me to digress for a moment to drive this point home. One afternoon in the early 1990s, I was hunting a tract of land on Bent Creek Lodge holdings about eighty miles to the south of my home in west central Alabama. This was an area I had hunted many times in prior years. It was early December, and we had a near failure of the mast crop that summer. In other words, virtually no acorns. As the fall progressed and the natural browse was dissipating, the deer were pounding the planted food plots and nearby bean fields. I had walked nearly a mile on a north, northeast compass path to the end of a slough that arched into a semicircle spanning half a mile from east to west, and joining the Tombigbee River on its east end. I was perched in a hickory at the west end of the water. The nearest field was nearly a mile to the south of my position. There was a 300-acre swamp to the north and east of the slough. As deer would leave the swamp, they filed around the end of the slough destined to arrive at the field well after dark. The wind was northwest at ten to fifteen miles per hour and was moving my scent completely out of the deers' path as they came around the end of the slough.

I took a doe in the first fifteen minutes in the stand at about 3:00p.m. She lay nicely concealed in some cane behind me and off to my left. A couple of hours later, a six-point rounded the slough and fed slowly up the hill toward me. I positioned myself for a shot but kept an eye out for other deer. Suddenly, I noticed the top of a sapling shaking violently directly across the slough and into the thicket on the other side of the water. I eased my binoculars up and could make out the top of the rack of a really impressive eight point. He had a massive body pushing 230 pounds, which is huge for an Alabama deer, and sported heavy sweeping main beams and long brow tines. His G2s pushed a foot in length. My heart pounded in my chest as I struggled to allow my brain to master my surging emotions. As the scene unfolded, I could see disaster in the making. The six-point had veered from his path and was now feeding on some smilax at the base of a dead tree ten feet in front of me. He was getting dangerously close when the big eight finally cleared the bushes on the opposite side of the slough. He walked, splashing as he came, slowly across the shallow end of the slough and as he cleared the water's edge, disappeared without pausing until he was hidden behind a large holly some thirty yards away. I had the perfect setup and timing to draw, but the six-point was now standing five feet from the base of the tree I was in. His head was down unaware of my presence, but it was just a matter of seconds until he smelled where I had climbed the tree. I could feel the stampede that was about to erupt. Sure enough, the six-point froze like a pointed bird dog, head down, snout forward, ears arched back. He held for about five seconds then bolted. The big eight jerked his head up, watched the young six-point trot off, and to my chagrin turned and walked away with the holly between us every vanishing step! I slumped back to a sitting position, took a deep breath, looked up at my Creator and smiled. "Thank you, Lord, for allowing me to witness such a magnificent display of your Creation."

Obviously, it was over. He had not been spooked, but he would be back later in the night and would doubtless smell my presence after I was gone. He would not return in the daylight hours again this season. I had done all my homework, stacked the deck in my favor, played my ace card, and came up lacking. Or so I thought. It was now nearing sundown, and I watched several more does and younger bucks splash through the water and disappear into the cane off toward the fields to the south where they would spend the night feeding.

I gazed at the ground below me and could see plainly the hook on the end of the rope I used to lift my bow. I heard water splash; then it stopped. Light was fading, but I could see the small waves emerge from the grass at the water's edge some forty yards up the slough. I eased my binoculars to my eyes and focused on the waves. There in the grass at the middle of the slough, stood the monarch. He waded down the middle of the slough for thirty yards, then as though on cue, turned and cleared the water's edge about nineteen yards in front of me. There was a dead fall with the base of the stump ten feet in front of this path. I knew if he continued on that path, I would have only seconds to get drawn. I was standing. My left shoulder addressed his location. My bow was out in position, and I gazed between the string and the limb. For what seemed an eternity, we both remain motionless. Then he took a few steps cautiously forward. His head disappeared behind the mass of roots, and I came to full draw. His chest cleared the tree, and he paused. I settled the pin, hesitated to confirm my site picture, and released.

He bolted in a semicircle and stopped five feet from the base of the tree I was in. By that time, I had another arrow in my right hand. He stood motionless, and I stood frozen, looking down from above. What seemed like a minute or two passed, but was likely only a few seconds. He suddenly eased down with all four feet folded underneath his body, like a dog lying in front of a fireplace. His head remained up and alert. He held that position for another minute. Then he eased his chin down to the ground, and his head slowly leaned over until his left main beam rested on the ground. I stood like a statue, the arrow still in my right hand, bow in my left hand, and my eyes glued to the magnificent animal below. I could hardly fathom what I was witnessing. After another long minute, I sank slowly to a sitting position, tilted my head toward the heavens, and said again, "Thank you, Lord. Thank you. Thank you. Thank you!"

What an afternoon!

Optimizing the Odds

With a bottleneck or point located near a bedding area and a food source in the opposite direction at least a few hundred yards away, a near perfect setup is afforded to the wise hunter catapulting his odds for success past the 90 percent mark.

As we discussed, the approach is as important as the spot itself. Not over hunting the spot is also paramount. Not many of these high quality spots exist and, therefore, when you find one, protect your treasure. You don't discuss them with your hunting buddies. You don't leave a ladder stand there to advertise the spot. I don't even tell my mother about them!

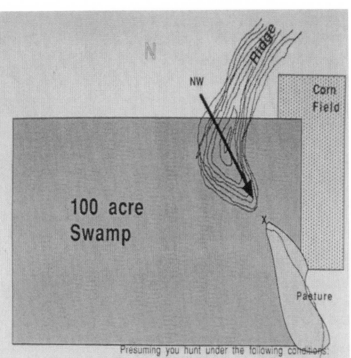

N

NW

Ridge

Corn
Field

100 acre
Swamp

X

Pasture

Presuming you hunt under the following conditions:
* No hunting pressure (No timber cruiser, coyotes, dogs, nor other hunters have walked through your stand site just before you hunt it.)
* With a north wind (i.e. cool weather)
* Good deer herd (one deer for 10 acres)
* Hunting for five hours

Likelihood of success:	Bow	Black Powder	Centerfire Rifle
A. Random chance, poor shooter (NE wind)	1 %	5 %	10%
B. Walking into the wind (NE wind)	5 %	15 %	20%
C. Adding point of a slough (NE wind)	15 %	25 %	30%
D. Adding pasturre to complete neck	30 %	40 %	50%
E. Hunt the neck on only a NW wind	40 %	60 %	60%
F. Adding food source on one side of neck	45 %	65 %	65%
G. Bedding area on other side of neck	55 %	70 %	70%
H. Adding ability to shoot well	70 %	80 %	85%
I. Hunting the stand infrequently	75 %	85 %	90%
J. When and how to take the shot	85 %	90 %	95%
K. Neck closer to the bedding area	90 %	95%	98%
L. You decide only to shoot a buck	15 %	30%	40%
M. Decide only to shoot a trophy buck	2 %	5 %	10%
N. Put the neck in heavy cover	4 %	8%	12%

Our spot is not just close to the bedding area, but now within it.
Take a look at the next graphic. Notice what happens to your odds for success when you decide to only shoot a buck? Do you see why I am not a trophy hunter when I'm bow hunting? I've taken as many real trophies (three and a half to six and a half-year-old bucks) with a bow as most of the famous hunters you've read about in America's outdoor journals. But I am still not a trophy hunter when I am bow hunting, because I rarely allow a doe to pass awaiting an old age-class buck, or any buck for that matter. When I'm looking down the barrel of a 300 Remington Ultra Mag™, this is not the case. But that is a very different adventure entirely (more on this later). Check out the next graphic displaying your odds of taking a trophy animal with a bow. The balance of the graphics show you other types of terrain features that can come together to comprise an excellent hunting spot.

Notice that through all this discussion, I have not mentioned expending efforts looking for tracks, rubs, nor scrapes. It's not that these "deer signs" aren't helpful, but they do not form the framework of where I hunt. If I see rubs and/or scrapes around the end of a slough or along an old logging road adjacent to a thicket, it helps me to know there are bucks using the area and that this is where they will be during the nighttime hours. But I do not hunt over these features.

Much like their food source, these deer signs mark the deer herd's nighttime activity pattern, not the movement pattern that allows me to encounter one during daylight hours. Oh, how many thousands of hours I wasted before finally figuring this out! The tracks were so fresh. The bark at the base of the rubs was still green. The steam was literally still rising from the fresh scrapes. I just couldn't understand why the deer rarely showed up. Little did I realize, they were sleeping peacefully a few hundred yards away, awaiting the safety of darkness. In light of this discussion, think about the corner of the last cornfield you visited. What did you find? Rubs posted on multiple saplings where the deer leave the woods to enter the field, and tracks forming a literal deer highway into the food source. When did it all happen? That's right. Under the cape of darkness. Allow your mind to follow these deer back to the thicket from which they slept awaiting the darkness. That is where success is born.

The Successful Hunter

Each year at our bow hunting schools, it would seem there are three typical hunter types who emerge.

1) A few, usually no more than two or three, will listen to what we say and be excited, soaking up the details and will go home and begin to apply what they learn to their own hunting clubs. I refer to them as hunters who will accumulate fifteen years of experience after fifteen years of hunting. These guys will become seasoned, successful hunters. The prime example of a person from this group is my dear friend and hunting buddy, David Stokes. David was one of those rare folks who just "got it" from the beginning. He had not deer hunted before, but one pass through what Ronnie and I had to say and he rapidly rose to be one of the most skilled whitetail hunters I know.

2) A few, again generally two or three, will take a surprisingly adversarial attitude that they know as much or more than the instructors. They are almost indignant about being told what comprise good hunting practices. Often these folks are average hunters with a lot of potential, but their pride stifles their ability to learn from others. They generally leave disappointed and will likely not advance much beyond

average skills because they are not able to learn from others' mistakes.

3) The bulk of the group eagerly listens to all we say, accept it as interesting and useful information, but unfortunately go home to make all the same old mistakes over and over again. I fondly think of this group as comprised of hunters who, after fifteen years of hunting, get one year's worth of experience fifteen times.

At the end of the introduction lecture on hunting basics at our bow schools each year, I use the following slide to illustrate how I profile the details a hunter should pay attention to in order to become a successful hunter. The most important factors are in large print at the top of the list and details that simply don't matter are in small print at the bottom of the list. You will be ahead of the vast majority of hunters if you pay attention to this order of factors and focus on the specifics that really make a difference. I think it provides a good visual barometer for summarizing the important details.

Becoming a Successful Hunter

Access to quality whitetail habitat

Hunting where hunting pressure is light
Hunting in the right place
Hunting when conditions are good
Dealing effectively with the wind
Hunting a good place infrequently
Learning to shoot accurately
Learning when to take the shot
Staying alert in the stand
The type of the tree stand you hunt from
The brand of bow you hunt with
The Camo pattern you wear
How high you climb to hunt
Type of bow (compound, recurve, longbow) you use
Quality of clothing you can afford
Arrow speed you can achieve
Avoiding UV brighteners in your clothing
Shooting heavy arrows
Type of broadhead you use
Shooting a heavy bow weight
Shooting a quiet bow
Phase of the moon
Using scents effectively

Dealing With the Wind

For the first ten years or so of my hunting experience, I struggled more with this concept than any other. I had a wonderful teacher in Ronnie Groom, but I just didn't get it. Looking back now, I must admit, I don't understand what it was about this concept that so confused me. It is so etched into my thinking now, that I can't remember a time when it was not clear. But I know there was such a time.

What Is the "Wind"?

Let me avoid the obvious mistake of assuming everyone knows, by simply defining what I mean by "wind." Consider here that these were the days before the Internet, before the PC, and before weather radios.

One morning I asked my wife to step onto the porch and "check the wind" for me. She had seen me do it hundreds of times. She disappeared for a moment and returned with, "Dear, there isn't any." Well, I knew it was possible to have a truly calm day with no wind, but I also knew the likelihood of that was really small. Frustrated, I stepped onto the porch and looked at the two-foot piece of white sewing thread I had hanging from an arrow tip that was itself hanging from a nearby tree limb a few yards from the porch. I identified the two mile per hour northwest "wind"immediately. It was so gentle, you could not feel it against your face. I walked back into the house and inquired, "Dear, what were you thinking? The wind is northwest at about two miles per hour." Now, you must realize here that we know wives have the innate ability to read any husband's mind, so the idea that she didn't know about the arrow/sewing thread setup just didn't cut it. I pressed the issue with, "But, dear, which way was the thread pointing?" And of course, I got, "What thread?" Because of the aforementioned ability, I knew she was just messing with me. It's like any item I can't put my finger on, I ask, "Dear, where's my so and so?" The standard response, "It's in your sock drawer." But just to humor her, I explained the setup. Without comment, she walked to the back door, stepped onto the porch, disappeared for a moment and returned saying, "If I tell you the string is pointing toward the Curry's (our neighbors across the street), which way is that?"

Arrow-based wind vane, before the internet.

Well, you get the point. When I say northwest, I
mean the wind (albeit sometimes very subtle) is
moving from the northwest toward the southeast.
One must also be careful about just where and
how you determine this wind direction. For
example, the reason for the arrow was simply to
have the thread hang from the tip of the arrow.
When the wind is really howling and the thread is
bouncing around in all directions including

straight up, it does tend to get tangled in the tree limbs. The weight of the arrow serves to hold the sewing thread down away from the limbs. When the wind is very gentle (say, less than four miles per hour), it will flow like a gentle river around large obstacles like a house and can give you a false reading of its direction. Tree lines and river edges are famous for creating eddies, turbulence, and rolling of the wind's basic direction fouling the hunter's best executed setup.

So, what I mean by "wind direction" is the basic reading you would get if you were standing in the middle of a fifty-acre field with no terrain or tree line features to alter the basic direction. This is what the weather service reports based upon check stations that are strategically located. But even this is wrought with problems at times. It is possible for the wind to "blow" with the primary mass of air movement being up a hundred feet or so above the earth's surface (caused by odd changes in air density). This has the untoward effect of "backwashing" every few seconds at the ground level. You may have a basic northeast wind direction, but the wind will come in a puff lasting several seconds, then it will pause, then backwash at the ground level for several seconds in the opposite direction. This has disastrous effects on a hunter sitting in a stand site fifteen feet off the ground relying on the basic wind direction for his setup.

A slowly approaching deer smells you well before he gets into a good shooting position because of these backwashes. So, all these variations in wind direction must be considered. Sometimes it is simply not possible to effectively hunt. If I can determine this before I enter the woods, I avoid fouling up a good spot under such poor hunting conditions.

Thermals

If all this confusion were not enough to discourage us, we must also remember that thermals add another element of surprise to the basic wind direction. I know, "What is a thermal?" you ask. During the night hours, the earth's surface cools considerably, regardless of the ambient temperature. The next morning as the sun rises, the earth's surface (and the air near it at ground level) warm quickly. This happens more rapidly in places like fields where the sun can strike the earth directly. As a result of this uneven warming, air movements that can be nearly straight up can occur. As the earth's surface cools in the afternoon, the reverse of this often occurs. Air that has been warm through the day cools and "settles" into low places along the earth's surface. If you are on the side of a hill, this downward thermal can move your scent down the hillside that may be completely counter to the predicted basic wind direction for the day. This happens most often from about sundown to dusk, the very time when a whitetail is likely to start moving. The morning's upward thermals can allow a deer that would otherwise have smelled you to literally walk underneath your scent when he appears to be directly downwind...not a bad thing indeed, but unfortunately not at all dependable.

As you can see, just understanding what the wind direction

means is tricky. Adding the effect of tree lines, rivers, fields, hills, valleys, thermals ...turbulence from whatever cause, can make for some difficulty in achieving a good setup for an ambush involving an animal with a legendary nose for danger.

Predicting Wind Direction

So, how do I "deal with the wind"? I first take my best shot at determining what the basic or prevailing wind direction for the day is going to be. In my early years, the arrow/thread setup was my basic wind vane. Later, I could actually find out tomorrow's prediction from the National Weather Service via a weather radio. That was a tremendous boost to my hunting success because I could go to my database (stored in those days on three-by-five index cards in a shoe box) and decide the evening prior actually where I would hunt the following day based upon (1) the time of year, (2) morning or afternoon hunting, and (3) whether I was bow or gun hunting all cast against the backdrop of the predicted wind direction.

Stand Site Approach

Let's say for example the wind prediction was to be from the northwest tomorrow morning. I would search the database for stand sites that could be effectively approached and hunted utilizing this northwest wind direction. The next morning, I would drive to a spot within half a mile southeast of that stand site. From there, I would walk toward the northwest, wind in my face, and climb the tree facing the northwest wind.

If this was a morning hunt, and the feeding area was off to the east and the bedding area off to the west, then I would expect the deer to be approaching from my right (east/food) coming from the feeding area moving into a bedding area where they would spend the daytime hours.

If, however, the feeding area was off to the west of where I was sitting, and the bedding area off to the east of where I was sitting, then I would expect the deer to appear from my left (food) moving toward the east (bedding). Obviously, deer don't always play by the rules, and they just might approach from the north or even try to slip in from behind me. Let it be known that I don't cull these confused misfits. They get the same medicine as those playing by the rules. If one comes near me, he gets a free ride to the lodge. But I think it is important to realize that you should be able to predict with some significant degree of accuracy which way the deer will approach your chosen stand site, and even learn to approximate the time they might arrive. This helps to ensure that you are paying attention and see the deer well before they approach your location. This allows you to prepare your body (stand up and address the direction) and prepare your mind (start deciding where you can effectively make the shot). This mental preparation helps curtail the effect of the natural anxiety/ excitement of executing that last thirty seconds before the shot.

Consider the second example above. The hunter could hunt this spot in the morning or the afternoon. Does this surprise you? Well, think about it. In the second example the deer movement is basically from southwest to northeast (morning) or northeast to southwest (afternoon). You have approached this site from the southeast, facing northwest. In other words, the morning and afternoon movement pattern here is perpendicular to your approach, hence it matters not at all whether you hunt it morning or afternoon. Your attention is focused in whatever direction you expect the deer to approach from, based upon the time of day. At least that is the way it appears on the surface; see "A South Wind Approach Won't Get It" below.

Movement Patterns

Let's consider another example. Picture a large bedding area along the north side of a hundred-acre stretch of mature hardwoods. To the south of the bedding area (on the opposite side of the woodlot) half a mile away sits a cornfield (or a food plot or a wheat field ...any food source). In the afternoon, these deer will be leaving the bedding area entering the north edge of the woods and will saunter south toward the cornfield where they will spend the night hours feeding. Now, understand that I know deer will sometimes "bed" inside the protection of a standing cornfield. More on that later. Here, we are attempting to visualize movement patterns where deer move in the afternoon from a primary bedding area toward a nighttime feeding area. To hunt these deer, you would need a north wind. The hunt would be an afternoon, not a morning. You would park near the cornfield (south of the woodlot), walk north facing the wind through the half mile of open hardwoods and setup near the edge of the thicket comprising the bedding area at the north edge of the stand of

hardwoods. You have assumed here that most of
the deer are not in the corn nor in the hardwoods
during the day. They are safely tucked away in
the thicket to the north of both. Once in the stand,
you expect the deer to come toward you moving
from north to south. So far, so good. Let's say
you shoot a deer and confirm the movement
pattern you had predetermined from the
information in your database. The following
season, you take another deer from this approach.
At this point, you label this spot as a site best
hunted in the afternoon utilizing a north wind.

How Deer Pattern Us

Now, let's take this exact same setup and see how
it might work in the morning. You check the
wind direction for tomorrow and it is predicted to
be straight from the north. The past two years'
success comes to mind, and you think, I believe
I'll hunt that spot tomorrow morning. You drive
to the cornfield, park your truck, and start the trek
northward to your spot. Where are the deer in this
scenario? The younger ones remaining in the
cornfield from the night before leave the
cornfield and move ahead of you into the woodlot
headed north toward the bedding area. Where are
the older age class deer? They had left the
cornfield well before daylight moving northward
through the woodlot toward the bedding area.

You now have the entire huntable herd ahead of you in the woodlot. As you move toward your stand site, you force the last of the deer into the thicket to the north ahead of you as you walk.

You walked to the spot walking into the wind and set up in the stand facing into the wind to the north. All morning, you wonder, Where are the deer? This was such a good spot. I saw nine deer last time I hunted here. Well, brace yourself. They are not going to show up. Then you really shoot yourself in the foot. You think, Oh, I see! They will be leaving this thicket in the afternoon moving toward the cornfield. I can get off work tomorrow afternoon, and I'll be here shortly after lunch. Indeed, you show up as expected and sit all afternoon, and what do you see? Nothing! What happened?

Think about what happened during the night following your hunt the prior morning. As deer leave the thicket, browse through the woodlot, feed in the cornfield through the night, then return to the thicket the following morning, many of them stumbled across the spot where you walked in, climbed up the tree, climbed down the tree, and walked out. You have left your scent scattered all through the area where the deer have moved through during the night hours. They simply avoid this area of the woodlot by approaching the cornfield via a different route, or worse, they just wait for the cover of dark to leave the thicket (i.e., they become nocturnal). The result is the same. You don't see squat that afternoon. You have now successfully buggered up a perfectly good spot for the rest of the season, and have nothing to show for it. The effect on the local deer herd is the same after hunting a spot whether or not you take a deer!

A South Wind Approach Won't Get It!

While you still have this scenario clearly in your mind, let's turn the geography around and make a point of the most revolutionary insight of all my hunting experience. In other words, the insight I'm about to explain about dealing with the wind, altered my hunting tactics more than any other over the ensuing twenty years. Let's leave the wooded timber where it is, but move the cornfield to its northern edge and the bedding area to its southern edge. In other words, we have simply reversed (north/south) the location of the bedding and feeding areas to north and south of the woodlot respectively.

For the sake of the discussion, we'll assume the area is pristine, not having been hunted this season. But now, to hunt the spot at the edge of the bedding area in the afternoon, we must drive to the cornfield now located north of the woodlot and walk toward the south through the woodlot to the edge of the bedding area, now located at the southern edge of the woodlot. To do so following our plan we walk into the wind to the stand where we hunt facing the wind ...a south wind. So, what do you suppose you would see if you hunted this spot in just this fashion once per season for twenty seasons? Nothing! That's right. Nothing. We have orchestrated a perfect setup, approached it from the perfect direction, and hunted it with attention, patience, and great skill. Yet, hunt after hunt, we see virtually nothing. I personally played this scenario out hundreds of times before I began to analyze the data in our mega hunting database. It became clear that hunting a south wind was dismally unproductive. After wasting thousands of hours hunting under these conditions, I begrudgingly gave it up. Today, if I check the wind direction to plan a hunt and find that it is south, I simply make other plans. I do not hunt when the wind is from the south, southeast, or southwest. Period. We'll explore this more in the chapter on reviewing the data. You may choose to violate the principle, and I do hope you enjoy the squirrels.

Deer Reading the Wind?

Before we leave this issue of wind direction, there is one additional factor I'd like to explore. I have read countless articles and books over the last forty years that recount the whitetail's ability to sense the wind and exploit it to the hunter's disadvantage. I'm afraid I have to tell you that this too is simply hogwash. Deer, albeit incredibly sensitive to their environment, do not have the ability to handle abstract thinking. They have absolutely no sense of what the wind is doing. They simply go where they want to go, allowing their eyes and ears to guide them. If along the way they encounter danger with their noses, they respond appropriately. But their nose does not predetermine the path they will take to get there. In fact, if you think about it a moment, my setups are designed to take only deer that are walking with the wind, or at best into a cross wind.

I've often told folks who attend our bow hunting schools (check out "http://www.BobSheppard.com" and follow the bow hunting school links), "If deer always walked into the wind, the ones in Alabama would be in Chicago by the end of the hunting season!" And while we are on the subject, with only a few exceptions, east and west winds carry about the same reputation as south, southeast and southwest. It's simply best to fish, work, or do some chores when you are facing any of these five wind directions ranging from east to west and across the southern horizon.

Let the Whining Begin!

I can hear the whining and wailing already. "This is fine for you ...a physician living a hundred yards from your lease, able to take off work whenever you like! But I have to go hunting when I can, not when the conditions are perfect." I would just remind you that I did not make the rules the whitetail lives by. I have learned to play by his rules to become an immensely successful hunter. You can do the same, or you can ignore them and enjoy the squirrels. It's your choice.

Characteristics of the Ideal Spot

There is a harsh reality concerning good spots that you are not going to want to hear. Namely, there are not many of them. And as though this were not enough, approximately half the good spots in the world are unhuntable in the daylight hours because they require a south wind (warm weather) to be approached and hunted effectively.

I would guess that by now you have at least some idea of what a good place might look like. You know that it is not likely situated at the edge of a food source. You know it will be near an edge (a point), perhaps even two edges (a bottleneck). You know it will be located near an area of thick cover (a bedding area, also commonly referred to as a sanctuary). You know it will need to be hunted utilizing a north wind (N, NE, NW). You know that it will have been hunted infrequently. You know that it will be in an area that has a solid whitetail population. You know that it will require you to approach it from a downwind direction. You know that it will likely require that you park in a different place than you usually do in order to approach it from a downwind position.

Terrain Features

From earlier chapters, you have likely gleaned that terrain features determine the basic construct of a good hunting spot, not the presence of "deer sign". Again, one must remember that hunting in my region of the South is limited to tremendous expanses of forested timberland...hundreds of thousands of acres in a single block. I realize that many of you confined to the Central and Midwest areas of the country simply don't have this concern. If you can find a tree to climb, it is likely near a movement pattern. But in our area, deer are free to wander aimlessly with few terrain features to restrict that movement. When a buck leaves a bedding area in the late afternoon, he may have a multitude of routes he can take to a favored nighttime food source. If you have two miles of edge bordering a bedding area, one has little chance of choosing the exact spot along that edge a deer will use as an exit point as he moves toward the food source. The same is the case the next morning. Just because a deer leaves a thicket at one spot in the afternoon, there is little chance he will enter the thicket at that spot the following morning...unless, of course, a terrain feature demands that he do so. Hence, terrain features often dictate where along an edge the successful hunter will set up his ambush. My personal favorite is a point.

Examples of points include the point of a body of water such as a sharp turn in a creek or river, one or both ends of a slough, the finger of a lake, the corner of an open expanse of land such as a field or pasture, a spot where one type of ground cover such as a clear cut juts into an open expanse of timberland, or perhaps a place where a long ridge suddenly drops to an end within an expanse of timberland. Any time you have two such points come near each other, a bottleneck is formed. Saddles along long ridges in mountainous terrain fall into this category, though as I suggested earlier, I have few, if any, of these in my area.

Bedding and Feeding Areas

Few points and bottlenecks are of much use should they not have the combination of a feeding area on one side of them and a bedding area on the other side. Again, it is important to understand that most natural deer movement is centered round basic survival involving safety and food. They spend their daytime hours in the safety of a bedding area (a thicket of some sort) and they move toward feeding areas (fields, new clear cuts, grain and legume patches, acorn flats, fruit sources, etc.) during the nighttime hours, hence their nocturnal reputation.

As you might guess, places where bedding areas fall adjacent to feeding areas can pose some major challenges to the hunter looking for a point or bottleneck between the two. Certainly deer do move at times for reasons other than this basic bedding/feeding cycle. For example should a coyote jump a deer, he will likely move from one bedding area to another and might well pass by your ambush point on the way. The same is true for rutting activity. I mentioned elsewhere my tactic of midday hunting confined to points and bottlenecks between large expanses of timberland on peak days like opening day, Thanksgiving, the day after Christmas, and New Year's Day. But few of my really good places limit my odds to these seasonal peak movement patterns. I am always in search of an ambush point between a bedding and feeding area. Should a coyote, the rut, or perhaps an unwitting hunting buddy push one by me, I certainly don't allow these to wander by unscathed. Inherent to this approach is the fact that I seldom hunt near a food source. As I state elsewhere, this is the last place I want to be for obvious reasons. This is the last place a deer is likely to show up during the daytime hours. At least that seems to be the case for the older ones. I realize this piece of wisdom is counter too much of what you have read, and may well be counter to your own hunting experience. Again, if you wish to move out of the league of the typical hunter, you must be willing to abandon his standard techniques.

More on Approach and Wind Direction

As I indicated earlier, choosing a spot is based primarily upon its terrain features and nearby bedding and food sources. However, wind direction forms a crucial part of the formula of success when hunting a spot. I have already focused a lot of attention on this factor elsewhere but would bring it to the surface again here for a slightly different reason. This is to help you decide if a spot you have located with all the above terrain, cover, food source, and bedding characteristics is indeed huntable. Now, what in the world could I mean by that? If a place has a nearby food source, borders a sanctuary/bedding area, offers a perfect setup for an ambush within a bottleneck, and is easily approachable, how could it not be huntable? Well, unfortunately about half the really good-looking spots you find will fall into this category. Basically if the spot requires you to approach it from the north and demands that you set up and hunt it utilizing a south wind, then it is for most practical purposes unhuntable. In other words, as we discussed in depth earlier, you can approach the spot with the wind in your face, hunt it facing into the wind, have the deer's path upwind of your position, yet see virtually nothing there on hunt after hunt. In the late winter and spring when I am scouting for the following season, should I locate a spot that requires a south wind to hunt it, I simply mark it off my list and never even enter it into the database. I know that the statistical odds of taking a deer here are so near zero that it isn't worth the effort to climb the tree.

Minimizing Hunting Pressure

Once again, I have worked this concept over elsewhere in this text, but it warrants repeating. The spot seldom hunted is the spot that seldom fails you. This is one of those concepts I have the most trouble driving home to hunters. And it seems those most resistant are the hunters who have enjoyed some modest success. They have engrained hunting patterns etched into their experience that have yielded an occasional deer, perhaps even a good one or two. These typically represent a favorite spot that, in fact, most often meets the criteria of a good spot quite nicely. The hunter may not have really understood what made the spot a good one, but tends to see deer there fairly routinely. Hunting the spot frequently during a season, and then from season to season slowly but surely diminishes its yield. But by this point in time, the hunter has enjoyed too many successful hunts here.

A friend of mine who has taken more than 500 whitetails with a bow has kept a detailed diary of his hunts for more than forty years! I asked him about this idea of overhunting a spot one day, and he immediately responded, "Let me show you something." He pulled out a ragged, worn logbook containing hundreds of hand entries of his personal hunting trips. He showed me the statistics revealing that nearly 70 percent of his successful hunts were represented by the first time he hunted a given spot each season.

The Deer Have Your Number!

But did you ever really wonder just how it is that deer do this? One afternoon more than twenty years ago, I was sitting in a strip of mature hardwood timber bordered on one side by the Tombigbee River and by a sixty-acre planted pine monoculture on the other side. The strip of timber was about sixty yards wide and spanned a distance of half a mile along the river. At the north end of the strip was a hundred-acre swamp. On the south end of the strip was a fifteen-acre wheat field. I was located about three hundred yards from the north end of the strip near the swamp and anticipating deer leaving the swamp in the late afternoon and using the narrow strip of mature timber as a travel corridor on their way to the wheat field where they would feed at night. This was in my early years of deer hunting and I did not yet clearly understand this concept of how deer pattern hunters. Two days prior, I had entered the strip to put up my steps so I could easily and quietly get set up when I planned the afternoon hunt. About sundown, I saw a pair of young does moving my way. As they neared my location, they stopped and stared for several minutes first one way, then another. After several minutes, they made a hard left turn and quietly disappeared into the planted pines. A few days later, I was telling my hunting buddy, Ronnie Groom, the story, and he said, "I have a better one than that." He recounted a similar experience from a few days prior in a similar strip further down the river. He had two young bucks walking together approaching his stand location (which he had assembled the day prior in anticipation of the hunt) when they suddenly walked over to the river bank, disappeared down the steep bank, stayed gone a couple of minutes, and then emerged back into the timber fifty yards past his stand location. These deer had been up and down this strip for two nights since we had placed our stands and had smelled where we left our scent on bushes, grass, tree bark, and the ground as we put up our stands. As I would come to realize after many years of this pursuit, the most important lesson for Ronnie and me lay not in the deer we saw, but rather in the ones we did not see. What we had witnessed were young deer avoiding our stand locations by detouring a few yards. The older age class bucks never made that mistake. They smelled where we had previously been, and they would avoid this stretch of timber in daylight hours for the rest of the season! Once again, we learn that the first time you hunt a spot in a given season is where your best odds for success lie. You should never venture into a place you plan to hunt past about August of a given summer. And what good does it do if you avoid an area and your hunting buddies stomp aimlessly through the areas you plan to hunt? Their ignorance will cost you many a successful hunt. There is no complete solution to this dilemma, but as I said elsewhere, my six-man club is broken into six parts. No one goes into my section after summer planting, and I don't venture into their areas. We plant together, work the roads together, paint the club house together, work on equipment together, but when it comes to hunting, I don't want any competition. The older deer will not tolerate it.

Protecting a Good Spot

In the early 1980s, I was a member of a large club sporting some 300 members and leases on more than 30,000 acres of land. Most of the hunters were dog hunters and lived for the weekend dog drives. I enjoyed these, but I was carving a niche as a solitary hunter in these early years. I had located a perfect ambush area near a wet swamp on the Sipsey River not far from our clubhouse. I slipped into the area one afternoon, quietly placed my steps, and ascended the tree. I had been sitting for about thirty minutes when I heard water splashing out in the swamp. A handsome buck sporting tall, dark antlers and heavy shoulders appeared from the brush about forty yards across a slough I was overlooking. I eased the .308 Cochise Lawson to my shoulder, settled the crosshair on his chest, and squeezed the trigger. He lunged forward, and I could hear him splashing water as he cut an arc off toward the river. I followed the blood trail about two hundred yards into the swamp but lost it in a place where there was too much water to track. I returned the next morning and spent most of the day searching for where he might have exited the swamp near the river but found nothing. The second night back at the clubhouse, I made one of those hallmark mistakes that human nature will not allow us to forget. At supper, someone asked me why I was wet, and I let it slip that I had shot. I explained that I planned to get a friend with a helicopter to fly me over the area the following day to see if I could see the deer's carcass or get some grasp on what he had done. Guess who was gathered to see where the helicopter would hover? Yep. All my buddies! I never saw another good deer in that area in all the years I hunted that club. The deer, by the way, had tried to swim the river, and from the air, we could see his shiny side lodged against a downfall midstream. Every time I look at his antlers today, I think of the hard lesson I learned about my good spots. When I locate a prime hunting spot, I would not even divulge its location to my mother!

Violating the Bedding Area

Many experienced hunters would tell you never to enter a bedding area or sanctuary. And there is considerable wisdom to this axiom. But I have made a hunting career of violating this dogma. First, let's make certain you know what a bedding area is. When I use the term "bedding area" or "sanctuary," I am referring to terrain with thick undergrowth and a closed overstory where deer spend most of their daylight hours. Examples might include clear cuts, hardwood shears, palmetto swamps, planted pine monocultures, and the likes. The thick undergrowth is pretty easy for most to grasp, but the closed overstory part might be a bit of a confusing concept to many. It has been my experience that deer seem to prefer not just thick areas, but thick areas that sun doesn't shine down into. The best example of this in my area of the South is the planted pine monoculture. When timber is cut in the rural South, the typical practice is to reforest that acreage with a monoculture of Southern pines. Interestingly, it takes about four or five years for those pines to get large enough to close the overstory, in other words large enough for the limbs to stop allowing sunlight to the forest floor. During the first couple of years after the clear cutting, deer tend to utilize these areas much like fields. In other words, they become a feeding area. As they become taller though, deer gradually begin to seek them out as bedding areas. From about year five to year fifteen, when these monocultures are first thinned, they form ideal protected habitat for whitetails to hide in during daylight hours. The key concept here is first to realize that deer are not just anywhere in the woods. Even during cold weather, at any one moment in time, more than 90 percent of a given area's herd is going to be sequestered within these bedding areas. The other 10 percent become the huntable portion of the herd. In warm weather, all but the youngest and most inexperienced deer (fawns and yearlings) will be within these bedding areas. I learned this early in my hunting experience, but it was not until later that I began to experiment with the shooting lanes cut into these bedding areas that I realized that the deer within these thickets still get up and move around some during the daytime hours but rarely actually leave the thicket. It is this movement within the bedding area that opens the opportunity for the discerning, diligent, and knowledgeable hunter. In addition, it's important to realize that this ambling around within the bedding area seems to take place all throughout the day, not just early and late. This makes hunting shooting lanes created within bedding areas productive even during the midday hours. More on this straight ahead in a moment.

I need to mention one additional variation of this bedding/feeding idea, and that is the whitetail's tendency to bed high in mountainous areas and feed low. This pattern is absolutely Greek to me. As I've suggested previously, a ridge in the area where I hunt is defined as any place that doesn't hold water following a rain. The land is f-l-a-t. I have no experience hunting mountainous terrain. So, I yield to those hunters facing its challenges.

Advanced Hunting Strategies

Most of our discussion thus far has been focused upon learning to recognize and locate ideal spots in the woods to set up an ambush. And indeed, this forms the framework of the successful hunter's approach. Much of the real work has been done at this stage. The rest is analysis of the data and plotting a finite strategy.

Scouting for Spots

Through most of February, March, and part of April each year, I walk the woods I will hunt the following season. It is during this time that I locate potential ambush points, bottlenecks, food sources, scrapes, rubs, and bedding areas, hence predicting where the deer will be in the daytime and where they will be at night. With the aid of aerial photographic maps, topographic maps, a compass, and a GPS, I walk out the relationships between these deer sign and terrain features. I leave my scent everywhere, but by the time the following autumn arrives, even the most wary whitetails will have returned to their normal feeding routines. As I walk and gather data, I keep notes on a notepad. In the 1970s and 80s

before the advent of the PC and GPS, I cataloged
this information on three-by-five-inch index
cards and utilized compass-derived coordinates
based upon known intersect points.

The old way...

Now, it is accomplished more efficiently utilizing
a computer database. Each potential stand site is
cataloged by a number in the database and
similarly marked on my aerial maps using
thumbtacks. Along with this number is also
stored basic information about the spot...for
example, its GPS coordinates, the general area
where the spot is located, whether it is likely to

be an early season bow site, a late season gun site, morning stand, or afternoon stand (more on this later), what wind direction it would be most effectively hunted with, to name a few. The database can be queried (searched) using any combination of these data elements. A graphic representation of the spot can be drawn and scanned in, or a digitized aerial photo can be stored showing what the place looks like from above. You can download a free copy of my stand site database program from my Website www.bobsheppard.com (or http://www.bobsheppard.com/BobSheppard.com/!

Lodge/Club Name	Rock Ridge Hunting Club
Area Name	Plateau Region
Field/Woods	Twin Pines Field or woods
Type Stand	bottleneck, clearcut, persimons, whiteoak acorns, American
Stand Name	Dead River Slough stand
Field Name	Lubbub Creek Field
Type Stand-Gun/Bow	Gun or Bow
Time to Hunt-AM/PM	AM or PM
Wind Directions	NE, N, NW, W, S, SW, SE, E
GPS Latitude	N 37° 13.968'
GPS Longitude	W 122° 06.418'

Stand Number 122

Rating 8

Comments:

The above entries are simply examples of how the data can be entered to give you an idea of how to get started.
The Club Name is self explantory.
The Area Name is meant to represent a specific area of the club where you hunt.
The Field/Woods distinguishes the spots you hunt into two basic categories... woods spots and field spots.
The Type Stand is a broad category of types of stands. In other words, a given spot in the woods may be good because it has a cluster of mature acorn producing whiteoaks, or perhaps a bottleneck between two creeks, etc.
Stand Name just allows you to name each stand site you may find.
The Field Name allows you to name each field.
The Type Stand-Gun/Bow allows you to categorize each stand site as being best hunted with a gun or a bow specifically.
Time to Hunt AM/PM means that some stands are best hunted in the morning, others best in the afternoon.
Wind Directions means the direction from which the wind would be blowing to most effectively hunt a particular stand site. The wind direction that you underline (under "Style" from the "Format" menu) represents the best wind direction for the stand site.
The GPS Latitude is the north/south position marker should you choose to use a Global Positioning System computer to mark your stand sites.
The GPS Longitude is the east/west GPS marker. Using a GPS hand held computer, you can return to a spot even in the dark (and find your vehicle again).
The Stand Number allows you to number each of your stand sites (an additional way of remembering your stand sites besides the GPS position marker and stand site name). Rating allows you to rate each stand site as to how productive you think it may be for producing deer sitings (1 being not very good... 10 being an excellent site).
The Comments is a place where you can make general comments about a stand location, write out directions of how to get to and from the stand location, or describe characterics of the stand such as what time of the season it would be most effectively hunted, etc.

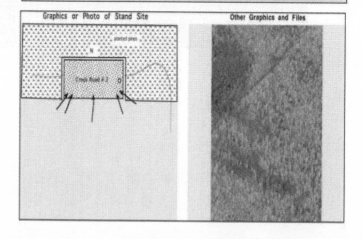

Graphics or Photo of Stand Site

Other Graphics and Files

For example, let's say it is October 23, early bow season in Alabama, and I am at Bent Creek Lodge and plan to go hunting tomorrow morning. I pull up a Web-based weather site that tells me what temperature and wind direction are predicted for tomorrow morning. I then query the database for all the sites I know about at Bent Creek that can be optimally hunted in the morning part of the day utilizing a northeast wind and that are well suited for deer feeding on food sources available in the early fall. From that list, I choose a site and plan the hunt. Had the wind been northwest, a totally different set of sites would have been reflected in the query list. Had it been January and peak of the rut, a very different set of sites would have been queried. In the early years, I found scores of places that could be effectively hunted (or so I thought) using east, southeast, west, southwest, or south winds. They were cataloged as well. With experience, I slowly realized these spots were completely worthless. I removed them from the database when I converted to a computerized version and these days, if the wind is not north (in other words, it is relatively cool), then I don't hunt. It's that simple. The statistical odds of taking a deer of any age is so poor, it is not deemed worth the effort. Taking a trophy is simply out of the question. In addition, every time I enter the woods, I am educating the deer in that area as they ramble the following night. They smell where I have been and not only tend to avoid that area, but tend to become more nocturnal in general. Therefore if the weather is not cold, I fish, squirrel hunt (not on my deer lease for obvious reasons), read, do yard work, write, or heaven forbid ... work. I would mention here that "cold" is relative. Cold in Alabama in October is 45 degrees. Cold in January is 25 degrees.

Older Age Class Bucks

Older age class bucks, like crusty old men have a bit of a tendency to become very stoic individuals. They are nocturnal, for sure, but when they move, their movement patterns do not tend to follow the rest of the herd's habits. They often isolate themselves in small parcels of the daytime sanctuaries, and as night approaches they venture off in another direction from the rest of the younger segment of the herd. These patterns are difficult to discern, but sometimes a scrape line leaving a thicket at a certain point can be a clue. Finding a multitude of rubs facing a thicket can indicate the same thing. But more often than not, I see one of these monarchs during the bow season, but he's out of range. When that happens, I make an entry in my database about this stand site and avoid the area until late January, or during the rut, then return with my .308 when the conditions are perfect for him to venture from the thicket a few minutes before dark.

When I was competing with the dog hunters in the late 1970s, I had a favorite spot on the river where the site was located on the backside of a thicket. To approach it required putting my boat into the river and running several miles by water. I would pull the boat up on shore, climb out, shinny up the bank and then up a tree. I could look down into my boat from the tree above. Other hunters would push deer into the thicket from the opposite open timber side, and I had cut three-foot wide shooting lanes into the thicket from my chosen tree in three directions about seventy-five to one hundred yards each. This of course, was accomplished the prior spring after the hunting season had lapsed. I took dozens of deer from this safe haven over a period of fifteen years, and none of my club members ever knew about the spot. They knew I was also a serious angler and just assumed I was fishing on the river.

The Wind Velocity Surprise

As I began to scrutinize the hunting/weather database, I noticed some unusual patterns of increased deer activity that I had never noticed in spite of years of diligent hunting. One of these centered around the wind. I was very aware that wind direction was a key component of my success methods, but I had never given much thought to wind velocity. My assumption had been that the quieter, the better. But as I analyzed larger subsets of the data, I noticed that quiet, still days produced few trophies, even when the temperature was relatively low. Curious about this, I did some multivariate analysis holding other variables within a fixed range and found an unexpected surprise. Not only did deer sightings and kills pick up noticeably with increases in wind velocity, but there turned out to be a pretty linear relationship between the two variables, other factors being equal. I had assumed that deer would move poorly when the wind was really howling. Quite the opposite turned out to be the case. The higher the wind velocity, the more the sightings soared and particularly with respect to older age class bucks. As I studied the phenomena, I wondered why, as a serious hunter, I had not noticed it. It made no sense. Assuming the data could not be deceiving me, I vowed to test the axiom. It didn't take but a few trips to the woods in twenty-degree weather with a thirty-mile-per-hour wind to solve the mystery. I simply couldn't stand it in a tree for more than a couple of hours under such conditions. During one of those few trips, however, I took a fine double-main-beam twelve-point scoring in the 150s. Molly was there to witness the spectacle in full HD.

Penetrating the Bedding Area

Over the years, I kept refining my attempts to get closer and closer to the thickets where I knew the trophies relaxed until dark. I kept thinking, There must be a way to get in there with them. I tried climbing high in trees at the edges of thickets and peering down into them. This was met with little success, and I was always uncomfortable at such heights.

Then one day, I was walking down a dirt road toward where my truck was parked. That particular section of the road traversed a wet swampy cane thicket near the river. With my bow in hand, I looked up just in time to see a massive eight-point step from the thicket a hundred yards from me, look down the road in the opposite direction from where I stood, then he leisurely ambled on across and disappeared into the thicket on the other side of the road. Suddenly, the light went on in my head. I could rent a big dozier with a shearing blade and create a "road" like this one into most any thicket. These wet, swampy thickets were bone dry in the midsummer months, and I had several of them on my lease. There was little more than bushes in these areas

and the landowner had no objection with my
clearing a lane through them. If I pushed the
"shooting lane" out several hundred yards long,
and placed a traditional four-by-four shooting
house on the south end of each one, I would have
a place where I could peer into the deer's bedding
area on the coldest, windiest day of the hunting
season.

*Shooting lanes created within a bedding area. Note deer crossing
at far end.*

If they had this tendency to move around within
their safety zone, this narrow gaze into their
domain just might be the ticket.The following
summer, I rented a D-4 Caterpillar (plenty big
enough to push through these bushes) and set out
to work. I pushed out three perfectly straight

shooting lanes into places where I suspected the deer were holding up during the daylight hours. The lanes were 300 to 400 yards long and about fifteen feet wide. I tried to create them in places where they ended near a road on the south end and abutted a creek or some other natural barrier on the opposite (north) end. Boy, had I hit pay dirt! That winter, I took five magnificent monarchs from these setups. I tried various tricks over the years like planting the lanes in wheat and other grains, but finally realized it made no difference. Just a pass with the rotary cutter once in the late summer, and I was set to go. They were cheap to build and easy to maintain. The deer never seemed to stay in the lanes for more than a few seconds at a time. They would typically step out, look one direction or the other (seldom both), then step on across and disappear into the thicket on the opposite side of the lane. One had to be really paying attention to hunt these places. I found that attaching a shooting platform for my gun, placing a small sliding window where I could close out the wind, sandbagging my 300 RUM into place, lighting a tiny propane heater, turning on my favorite audiobook on my iPod, pouring some hot coffee, and settling back to a pecan cookie made for some really fine relaxation. I would sit gazing for hours down this window into these monsters' bedroom. I found that it made little difference what time of day I hunted. I took just as many big deer through the midday hours as I did early and late in the day. The colder the better, and the more windy the better! And since I was approaching and sitting on the south end of these big thickets, but never venturing down the lane nor into them, I could hunt the sites repeatedly without altering the deer's tendency to move around in the daylight.

Shooting lanes in a swampy bedding area

Dealing with the Distances

I soon found it to be a bit tricky to simultaneously judge the deer's antler quality and the distance to him, and to accurately place the shot when he was much beyond about 250 yards. My .308 was out of the question. It did not have the trajectory to hit the animal with any consistency at extended distances, and even when it did that far down range, I had a half-day tracking job finding the deer, often with no blood trail. And these thickets are no place to be crawling around. We have some really fine rattlesnakes in this part of the South, even in the winter months. I moved to a Colt-Sauer bolt action 30–06 and utilized really hot hand-loaded cartridges and this helped, but shooting accurately beyond the three hundred yard mark was still a pain.

I tried cutting small saplings and laying them across the lanes at 300, 350, and 400 yards. This helped but still did not completely solve the problem. Finally a friend of mine, Craig Thornton, bought one of Remington's 300 Ultra Mag™. He said the recoil was awful but that it would reach out and touch them at the 400-yard mark with a flat enough trajectory to not overshoot those in the 150to 250-yard range. Craig was always a magnificent shooter, and I knew he had an odd look on his face when he was relating the gun's merits to me. Then, handing me the gun, he said, "Here's your Christmas present for this year. I hope you enjoy the punishment!"

Shooting house window...from the outside

Shooting house window...from the inside

134

The first time I pulled the trigger on this behemoth, every dirt dauber nest in the shooting house fell, and the recoil broke the front window out of my shooting house and nearly broke my nose. I think the only reason the scope didn't whack my brow was that it had slammed into the top of the window bracing on the way up. Whoa! This was some hot beast of a gun. I could now clearly see what made the "short magnums" popular. I tried a few more rounds but agreed with my friend that this rascal was more than I could handle. It was a Kevlar™ stocked, relatively light sporter version of the rifle. As I entered the house, my wife, Brenda, greeted me with a kiss as she passed in the hallway and said, "How'd shooting the canon go?" I just winced at the thought and shook my head. Then from wisdom only a woman can conjure, she offered, "Why don't you fill it up with lead?" I paused, gazing thoughtfully down the hall of our hundred year-old home. "Lead?" Perfect! I was off to the sporting goods store where I purchased a twenty-five-pound bag of number nine birdshot. I took the butt cap off the 300's stock and poured about eleven pounds of the lead shot into the hollow Kevlar™. I then removed the barreled action and filled the hollow forestock with another few pounds of the shot. I then poured epoxy down into the forestock lead shot, placed a piece of wax paper over the epoxy, and followed with a thin sheet of aluminum over the wax paper. I bolted the barreled action back into the stock and waited for it to dry. Giving the epoxy plenty of time to solidify, I took it back apart, removed the wax paper and aluminum sheet, and replaced the barreled action. I could easily pass a dollar bill between the epoxy formed lead shot and the barrel, all the way to the chamber. I had a gunsmith square the bolt face, lighten the trigger to about 2.2 pounds, and I was off to the range again.

Just don't forget to put the lead in the stock!

The recoil was tamed to barely that of my 30–06 and with heavy handloads of Reloader™ 22 and 165-grain Nosler Ballistic Tips™, I was able to achieve 1.8-inch groups at 300 yards! I had developed a clear solution to the distance problem. The gun looks so innocent that I can't help but smile every time someone picks it up. It looks like a standard out of the box Remington 700 Sporter (which it is). And when you drive a 165-grain bullet through a whitetail at well over three times the speed of sound, he typically runs exactly one yard. Tracking is rarely necessary.

The 300 RUM will reach out to the ends of the shooting lanes.

Leveraging the Wind

During my years of working with the commercial hunting operations, I spent a lot of time helping them analyze the data we were collecting to allow them to optimize the hunting operations for their customers. After all, if their guests see deer and follow through with successful harvests, everyone leaves happy. And they happily return the following year (more on this in the chapter about habitat management). One of the things we noticed early on was that certain fields were not very productive. Being so cognizant of the wind's effect on hunting success, we realized the shooting houses on fields needed to be set up to take the best advantage of a given wind direction. After all, when someone books a hunt at a commercial hunting lodge, they have no control over the wind. So having a field setup with your scent blowing across the field is pretty disheartening, not to mention, counterproductive. Therefore the existing fields were corrected and new fields were built with wind direction being the primary issue in their construction. This inevitably means you have some "north wind fields" and some "south wind fields." That way, when the lodge guides are placing their hunters, the wind direction for that day can be matched to a field's setup. As you have already likely surmised, we learned early on that hunting during relatively cool weather (north wind) is more ideal than hunting during warm weather (south wind).

Hunting South Wind Fields

All this lead me to suspect there would be some older age class deer that tended to feed in these south wind fields predominantly at night, meaning they never get themselves killed because hunters are forced by the elements of nature to hunt under less than ideal conditions and even though the fields are optimized for the given weather conditions. I mused, Wonder what would happen if I built myself a ground blind and hunted some of these south wind fields from the opposite end utilizing north wind conditions? Whoa! I had hit another home run. Granted, it was not quite as comfortable sitting in the weeds with a blustery freezing wind in my face, but the results were nothing short of stunning. I saw deer on these fields that none of the lodge's regular customers ever saw, and for obvious reasons.

The Bane of the Mornings

I love to talk to people and having spent a gazillion hours at commercial hunting lodges afforded me the opportunity to pick a lot of hunters' brains. I love finding out what makes them tick, why they love this sport so much. In addition, another quirk of this experience surfaced. Hunters, who can afford to pay several hundred dollars per day to hunt, often are savvy in more than just income production. They are serious thinkers. They like analyzing their hunting experience as much as I do. But one of the questions they frequently ask me is, "How successful are you at taking deer in the mornings?" The question is loaded, of course. What I've found is that most hunters find that patterning deer for success in the mornings is more difficult than in the afternoons. At first, I thought it was an odd question, because I knew that I tended to kill more deer in the morning than the afternoon. But after some reflection, I realized that I had struggled with this in my early years as well. Remember, I started deer hunting by glassing large bean fields, which is pretty much an afternoon venture. There would be ten times as many deer in these fields in the afternoon compared to the morning. The recognition of the bedding area concept is the key to solving this problem. As we have discussed, deer tend to spend their daytime hours resting in thickets (bedding areas) where we cannot easily venture. As night approaches, they start to move from these domains into adjacent open timber and later to nearby fields where they will feed through the night hours. As dawn approaches the next morning, they reverse this movement pattern, returning to the safety of the thickets where they will spend the day. With this in mind, I began to analyze the movement pattern associated with each of the spots I had identified in my database and quickly noticed that some spots tended to be good "morning stands" while others were good "afternoon stands." From my experience observing these movement patterns, I slowly began to piece together what was going on. As you might imagine, deer that leave a bedding area and wander toward a feeding source in the afternoon, will, in general, take a similar path back into the bedding area as daylight approaches the following morning all things being equal. However, during the hunting season, things are no longer equal. We, as hunters, have the tendency to approach our hunting sites with little knowledge of these movement patterns and more often than not push the deer right back into the bedding area ahead of us when approaching our morning stand sites. As I began to study these movement patterns and unravel those associated with each of my stand sites, I became aware of very different approaches necessary when hunting a site in the morning versus the afternoon. But wait! Didn't I already show you that one should hunt a stand with a particular ideal wind direction and that we should try to always walk into the wind when approaching that particular spot? It becomes apparent that this simply isn't possible when hunting a spot morning and afternoon. As a result, one must compromise either his approach or his location once in the stand, neither of which leads to effective hunting. So, what is one to do with this dilemma? The fact is, you must choose between the two approaches for a given site. Few sites can be hunted effectively in both the morning and afternoon. Once I find what appears to be a good spot (based upon the criteria we have already established), I usually try the site using the ideal morning approach first. After a couple of hunts yielding no success (Remember, this requires two seasons!), then during the third season, I trying hunting the spot using an afternoon approach. More often than not, one or the other will be a standout winner. I label it that way in my database and stick with that approach during all future seasons.

Using Water to Your Advantage

Before I stumbled upon the Rokon™, I devised a way to carry my small four-wheeler on a rack on the back of my truck because I hate to deal with pulling a trailer. During my late winter/spring scouting, I would often locate a good place that was protected by water or perhaps would require an approach from water to effectively hunt. For this job, I rounded up a tiny plastic boat that I could carry on my truck, then drag through the woods with my four-wheeler or Rokon™ to the water's edge, take the deer, then float him back across the water and drag him in the boat back to my truck. Yes, these approaches require more effort, but then that's why I refer to them as advanced hunting strategies.

The four-wheeler/cartopper boat combo was hard to beat for getting to difficult to reach places in the early days of my hunting.

The Rokon™ (www.Rokon.com) will go places a four-wheeler can only dream.

Some of the information in this chapter will be cross-covered in the chapter on the experienced hunter. That's just as well; this is often difficult information to master and bears repeating.

The "Peak Days" Phenomena

During the years when I was competing with several hundred dog hunters, club members were beginning to learn that I was wearing the deer herd out with my .308. I tried to leave no trace of where I had hunted in the woods, but the hunters would watch to see where I parked my truck, figuring I must be hunting somewhere in the area. They would wonder through that area looking for any evidence of my favored hunting spots. With this pressure, a pattern began to unfold. I would park my truck, walk half a mile into an area, but notice that I seldom saw deer during the peak early morning hours. But I was persistent and would frequently remain in my stand through the lunch hours. After taking several deer between nine a.m. and noon, I suspected something different was going on. However, it wasn't consistent. Then it hit me. The deer movement in the late morning hours that I was witnessing was not normal feeding movement. It was stimulated by other hunters climbing down after a short time in their stands, and beginning to walk and "scout," as they called it. In other words, they were bored, having seen nothing, and so they would climb down and start to ramble aimlessly through the woods. This activity moved deer around, and I was setup in ambush spots and caught the movement patterns they unknowingly caused. Once I noticed the pattern, I set about to fine tune this predictable daytime movement. I rationalized that there would be certain days during the hunting season when the woods would be full of other hunters, most of whom had little idea of where or how to hunt. Normally, their presence in the woods would push the herd toward nocturnal movement patterns and make them really difficult to take using the usual feeding movement patterns. Following this logic, I marked several of these potential days on my calendar. Opening day of the gun season, Thanksgiving Day, the day after Christmas, and New Year's Day brought virtually guaranteed success. I would wait until mid morning to leave my home, then drive to my club, park my truck, and walk to one of these ambush spots often comprised of narrow bottlenecks situated between large expanses of wooded timber. I would sit patiently through the midday hours. Rarely did one of these peak days pass without my having met with success, fostered by my unwitting hunting companions' impatience.

Avoiding the Food Sources

I think you are beginning to see that I rarely, if ever, intentionally hunt near a food supply. This is indeed the case. I realize this is counter to much of what you have read in the hunting press for the last fifty years. But this understanding of whitetail behavior, perhaps more than any other, has become the centerpiece of my hunting success. Starting at the edge of a lush food plot and allowing my eyes to see the young deer as they arrived and using my mind to then backtrack them to their daytime haunts formed the basis of a life's pursuit. It has not been an easy pattern to unravel, but tracing these young deer's movements from feeding back to bedding areas allowed me to finally begin encountering the older age class animals at their source. And if we are honest with ourselves, these animals are the ones we treasure and long to see. I watched my hunting companion, Ronnie Groom, drag trophy after trophy from the woods before I finally began to have the light come on to this wisdom.

What Is a Trophy, Anyhow?

And now that I mention it, what is a trophy whitetail? Well, you know the standard answer: "It is what you believe it to be." Perhaps. But I think a slightly more precise definition would be a three and one half year old animal or better, sporting the best set of antlers your geographic area has to offer. In west central Alabama where I hunt, that is an animal scoring between 120 and 160 B&C (or P&Y). Having taken more than a hundred of these unforgiving animals, I have never seen a whitetail in the wilds of this area that I thought would be an honest B&C book entry. They exist, but only one or two per decade appears from among the millions of whitetails taken in this area. Should I ever encounter one of these rare and magnificent animals, you can bet I will stare him in the eye with controlled intent until his ticket is punched for a free ride to the lodge. If I lived in Kansas or Iowa, you can bet, the table displaying my efforts would look quite different indeed. In the meantime, I am content to take the best of what our area has to offer ...unless of course, a young nanny should arrive first! I've said before and I'll say again, "With a bow in my hand, I am no trophy hunter!" The first nanny to arrive gets the prize.

Tracks, Rubs, and Scrapes

As I work through the late winter and spring in search of good hunting spots for the coming season, I think it is important to understand just what it is that I'm looking for. I am rarely, if ever, looking for deer sign, per se, although I take note of it when encountered. My scouting centers around terrain features and not deer sign. The reason for this is simple but often poorly understood. Most deer sign (tracks, rubs, and scrapes) is made at night by nocturnal animals. This revelation should not come as a surprise to us, but often it does. When I observe a lot of tracks, a line of scrapes, or a cluster of rubs, I think of those as being similar to food sources. They signify that deer are nearby. They give us some sense of the age structure of the deer herd in the area, and the scrapes and rubs give some hint of the size and quantity of bucks in the area. But they rarely signal a place to hunt. Scrapes, for example, are often found along an old logging road or along the entrance to a field. They tell me a buck is in the area and that he travels in this general direction every evening after dark and likely again the next morning before daylight in his daily rutting routine. Still most of this activity happens at night. The next time you stand looking at a fresh scrape, pause for a moment and think, Now where is the nearest thicket to this scrape? Find yourself a suitable ambush between that scrape line and the thicket. Why wait for the animal where he is most likely going to arrive well after shooting hours? I may be completely wrong about this, but I think most rubs are made in the evening hours of the day. When you find a cluster of rubs, just stand and look at them for a moment. Which way must the deer have been facing when he made them? Now, think about it; if he made them in the evening, from what direction did he arrive here? His daytime haunt is behind you! So, don't place your stand where you see the rubs. Backtrack him to the thicket where he is spending his daytime hours. It is there where success is brewed.

Scents, Grunting, and Rattling

I realize I'm on thin ice here, but I just have to tell you the truth. Ronnie and I were leaning into the sofa at a hunting lodge one evening many years ago reminiscing about the tumultuous years of our teenage children. He said, "My son was wanting this pickup truck that was well out of his and my means, and I was trying to explain that it just wasn't feasible. But he wasn't buying my argument. Finally in the midst of the frustration, I said, 'Right now, while you know everything, why don't you go ahead and make all of your life's important decisions?'" I echoed his sentiment, but then we remembered just how much like us these teen wizards were. We become dogmatic about gadgets and shortcuts, more often than not, based on little fact. We simply want them to work. As you might guess, as a physician with nearly two hundred semester hours of biology, chemistry, math, and physics behind me, the manufacturers of cover scents don't have to explain the adsorbing (as contrasted to absorbing) properties of such substances as baking soda. There is no question that they work, at least chemically speaking. When applied in a hunting environment, I don't think they hurt a thing, with the possible exception of your wallet. I think it was Ben Lee, the late and famous turkey hunter, who once said, "If you could make a living buying cow urine in fifty-five-gallon drums and have people demand it by the ounce, pour it out on the ground, then return for some more, wouldn't you think that's a pretty good business?" There are a few curious deer in most deer herds, particularly if there is not much hunting pressure.

I have seen deer respond to grunt calls, and there is little doubt that they will, on occasion, cause a curious deer to venture close enough for a shot that would not have otherwise materialized. Contrast that with the number of deer people run off fumbling with a pack full of gadgets, and I do not think the net value holds much water. In Alabama where I hunt, a good pair of rattling antlers will be toothpicks by the time something responds to them. And yes, I have been to Texas. And yes, these animals will come to rattling like a cat to a mouse eating cheese. But remember what I told my Texas guide after the first few days observing his herd? "If these animals were moved to Alabama, they would all be dead by Thanksgiving!" Virtually all the curious animals on my lease have been dead for many years. If your hunting lease contains a bunch of these highly pressured beasts, then I suggest you get down to the basics and forget the Outdoor Channel™ dreamland. You and I are not going to be hunting these unpressured, protected Utopian haunts any time soon.

In summary, the hunter who is applying advanced hunting strategies will have taken a very analytical approach to identifying and locating ideal hunting spots. He will have taken great pains to approach these spots facing into the wind to have remained undetected. He will be a disciplined hunter who will avoid the temptation of hunting a spot when the conditions are not perfect, or nearly so. He will have avoided over hunting a good spot. When hunting fields, he will have located the field in the right place when he built it, set it up to hunt effectively with a north wind, and to have approached it so as to remain undetected. He will hunt with his brain rather than relying on gadgets and crutches.

Habitat and Herd Management

Food Plots

At first, I was hesitant about even including this chapter because there is so much on TV and in magazines covering the details. Then I was watching a program on the Outdoor Channel™ one afternoon on "how to construct food plots in the South." They illustrated in great detail the nuances of food plot development from how to get soil samples to what to plant once established. But nowhere in the documentary did they divulge the most important aspects of food plot development. So if you would allow me to just ignore the basics of what most everyone seems to already know about habitat management and come at this from somewhat of a different angle. To rent a dozer big enough to establish a food plot runs about $100 to $150 per hour and takes about ten to twenty hours depending upon the number and age of stumps remaining to be cleared. You can readily see that this is a costly venture even when you do much of the work. Therefore, would you not think it wise to make absolutely certain you have it setup right and located in the right place before you spend such funds? Okay. What is the "right place"? And what is the "right setup"?

To answer these questions, allow me to digress a moment. In the early 1980's I worked with some large commercial hunting lodges to help optimize pay by the day hunting as a viable business model. In doing so, we developed some computer software that would allow us to fine-tune the operations by tracking certain aspects of the process. For example, one of the South's most successful operations, Bent Creek Lodge (www.BentCreekLodge.com) plants several hundred food plots across its massive 45,000-acre spread each year. Early on, they wanted to know if there were characteristics of a field that would make it particularly well suited for their customers both seeing and taking whitetails on a regular basis. After all, if it costs the same amount to establish two fields, and we find after five seasons that one field had a four-fold higher statistical likelihood of a hunter taking a deer from it on a given day, we would certainly like to know what that field's characteristics were. So we meticulously catalogued the details of each field from their inception. We tracked things like the number of tons of lime each field required, the amount of fertilizer they required (based upon soil tests), the size of the fields, the shape of the field, what grains and legumes they would grow, what kind of timber bordered the field, from what direction the field was approached, what wind direction best suited the field once approached, and on and on. Of course we confirmed much of the expected dogma concerning pH and fertilize requirements, but a surprise surfaced when we began to notice that certain fields were consistently producing several times as many deer sightings as seemingly comparable fields. Analyzing the data more discerningly, several new facts emerged. Counter too much of the TV hype, the larger the field, the more deer sighted given all other characteristics were the same. The ideal size seemed to be about three to five acres. The upper size range was limited not in sightings, but rather how far the average hunter could reasonably shoot. A five-acre field, regardless of what shape you form it will push the limits of the average shooter. So why build it larger? But we noticed early on that small plots, particularly those half an acre and less had a dismal track record of producing sightings, and much less kills. Rarely was a trophy animal taken from these tiny plots. That doesn't mean the deer don't use them. They do. It's just well after dark, making it pretty useless from a hunting perspective. So, if you have the choice of building four one-acre plots or one four-acre plot, just remember that at the end of ten years, you will have spent the same amount of money and will have seen approximately one third as many deer on the small plots! And that fact is based upon more than 35,000 hunting trips, not just my anecdotal belief. But, believe it or not, that is not the most important characteristic of a field's statistical odds of producing deer sightings! The most important characteristic actually has nothing to do with the construct of the field itself, but rather where it is located and how you approach it. Allow me to explain. Let's say you have a hundred acres of wooded timber and were trying to decide where on the acreage to establish a single four-acre food plot. How would you decide where to place it? In the middle? On the west side? Along the north border? Well, you would want to take two factors into account: (1) From what direction are the deer going to approach the field? (2) From what direction are you going to approach the field? The answer to question number one should be "the north," and the answer to question number two should be "the south." Therefore, you should place the food plot a couple of hundred yards into the woods from the south border and you should approach it from the southern edge of your property. That would mean that when you get to the field, the shooting house should be located along the southern edge of the field and you should hunt facing north, northwest, or northeast...but basically north. You want no other roads going near the field and human activity near the field to remain at a minimum, even outside the hunting season, and certainly during the hunting season. Fields located near large creeks, rivers, pastures, roads and human activity like boat ramps and campgrounds are destined to perform poorly. You should never hunt the field unless the wind is blowing from the north, northwest, or northeast. Did I say, never? This arrangement would stack the statistical odds of success maximally in your favor ...and at no additional cost! You may ask, "But what do I do when the wind is from the south?" I think, by now, you know my answer to this question. Do you like to bass fish?

Cut Them Some Slack!

Having said all this, just bear in mind that commercial hunting operations do not have control over the wind direction and as a result, they have intentionally built some of their fields expressly for hunting south winds. (Read the section called Hunting South Wind Fields in the chapter on advanced hunting techniques for more detail.) They realize this is less than ideal, but neither they, nor you, have much choice in this matter. You have paid your money, and they want you to have the best odds possible under the conditions, dismal as that may be. So don't fuss at them when they set you up on the "wrong" side of a field in warm weather. They are doing the best they can under the circumstances. In addition, they often have their land lessors determine the location of flood plots before they obtain leases on some of their land holdings. In these cases, they work with what they have. On their own land holdings, they have pretty much incorporated the principles I discuss here.

Shooting Lanes or "Senderos"

Fields that we call "food plots" have become the standard approach to hunting in the South as well as much of the rest of the country. Afternoon hunting on these plots is historically far superior to the mornings for reasons that have eluded me. I have described in some detail my "shooting lane" approach to hunting sanctuaries and I'd like to expand that concept a bit here as well. The idea is to use a dozer to push a long roadlike lane through thick, heavy ground cover. This may be a swamp, a clear cut, a hardwood shear, a planted pine monoculture or other thick terrain within which a deer will tend to spend its daytime hours. The approach to placement of these shooting lanes (commonly called senderos in the West) is the same as those for establishing fields. You should always approach them from the south side. They should be laid out to run basically north/ south (for example, northeast to southwest or northwest to southeast, or north to south). The shooting house should be sitting on the south end of the lane facing toward the north end. The lane should be about twenty feet wide, though this can vary a bit depending upon the lane's length. I like mine to be about fifteen feet wide at the south end, span about 300 to 400 yards, and gradually widen to about twenty-five feet at the far north end. They require approximately half the cost of that of establishing a field and do not require soil tests, liming, nor planting, although we tried all these treatments on our lanes. We found no gain in sightings by planting. We just run the rotary cutter over the lanes once in late summer, and with a little limb trimming along the edges, they are ready to hunt.

Maximizing Edge

Perhaps the concept to keep foremost in your mind when managing a piece of land for optimal whitetail production is to maximize edge. Examples of edge include roadsides, the edge of fields, and the border between two stands of timber of differing ages, fence lines, and streamside management zones (called SMZs). It is along these edges that deer find much of the favored browse they depend upon for growth and development. However, just bear in mind that attention to these edges actually decreases the odds of taking a deer from your food plots. These edges are generally not huntable spots, and deer tend to frequent these edges at random, meaning they will, on any given day, pull a portion of the herd's attention away from your food plots. So even though they maximize your land's carrying capacity, there is a price to pay. Just keep this in mind when you start spending money on fertilizing roadsides.

Controlled burning remains one of the habitat manager's finest and most cost-effective tools in producing quality whitetail habitat. Because of liability issues, burning has become more of a hazard in recent years, but when done correctly, it is quite safe. Most areas have a "burn permit" office often handled by the soil conservation office in your area. You can give them a call, and they will walk you through the necessary steps to get you safely burning your timberland during the winter months. Burning returns minerals to the soil to be utilized by other fresh browse and increases the pH of the soil by returning $CaCO_3$ (calcium carbonate...lime), hence increasing the soil's productivity.

Keeping Data

The management of a whitetail herd's habitat goes hand in glove with the management of its animals. There are basic pieces of data you need to keep track of when trying to manage a deer herd, such as average body weight for a given age class and gender as well as antler development for a given age class animal. I have provided two electronic database programs to make this process easy, one for small hunting clubs or groups, and one for a more commercialized operation. Go to my Website (www.BobSheppard.com) and follow the download links (http://www.bobsheppard.com/BobSheppard.com.

Leasing Land for Hunting

Many years ago, it was possible to work out really good leases with landowners, but these days, there is little opportunity for the leasing hunter to do much other than sign his name at the bottom of whatever document he is offered. But should you have that option, allow me to give you a little advice about how to arrange your lease's wording. The most important thing about a lease is its stability. In other words, deer herd management is a moving target. A group of hunters can pick up a lease, spend five years shooting virtually nothing, while allowing the herd to mature into a balance of young and mature animals with a range of age classes. Suddenly in year six of the lease, the landowner realizes he has a fine place and doubles your lease, or worse, leases it to the highest bidder. You have spent your time, effort, and money developing a quality habitat only to have the landowner cash in on your work. I have had this happen more than once in the last thirty years. With that in mind, allow me to share a piece of wording I have incorporated into my lease agreements that gives the lessor/hunter some protection:

> The length of the contract shall be three years according to the following terms. Within one month of the first year's lease anniversary date, the Lessor agrees to negotiate the fourth year's lease terms with the Lessee. Within one month of the second year's lease anniversary date, the Lessor agrees to negotiate the fifth year's lease terms with the Lessee. According to this pattern, each year thereafter, the Lessor agrees to negotiate the lease terms with the Lessee for the year to begin approximately two years from the lease anniversary date. Should the Lessor and Lessee not be able to negotiate a mutually agreeable lease allowing the lease to continue, then the lease shall be cancelled two years from that lease anniversary date. To more

clearly define this lease concept let's consider the following example: Let's say, for example, the initial lease begins on 7/31/95. This lease would extend from 7/31/95 to 7/31/98 (three years). On approximately 7/31/96, the Lessee and Lessor would negotiate the lease agreement terms for the year beginning 7/31/98 to 7/31/99 (the fourth year of the lease). This pattern would simply be repeated each July.

The idea here is to avoid the dilemma of building up a herd and then having the lease pulled from you. According to the above terms, you always have a two-year window to harvest deer you have let walk, before the lease can be terminated.

One of my larger leases has an additional feature you might consider. At the beginning, the landowner and I negotiated an annual rate of increase of a few cents per acre in addition to the above provisions. With that in place, he and I were content to just let the lease go. After more than twenty years, we have never altered the agreement and the lease amount is about in the middle of the area average per acre. He's happy, and I have a stable lease we've enjoyed for two decades.

Acquiring Land for Hunting

After many years and more money than I'd like to admit spent pursuing the whitetail, I'd like to offer some advice for the young hunters across America with respect to the most cost effective ways to approach deer hunting. I realized early on that buying enough land on which to effectively hunt was not within the reach of most hunters, myself included, or so I thought. Therefore, I took the hunting lease approach to deer hunting as did most hunters across the country for the last thirty years. But in recent years, I have stumbled into a different, but quite effective approach to actually buying quality whitetail habitat. To have enough land to effectively manage for whitetails requires at least a thousand acres unless you fence it and even this is quite expensive running about $20,000 per mile just for the fence. But as I analyzed the data on field development described above, I began to realize that if it is deer hunting and not deer management you are chasing, then there just might be another approach.

If you build a very isolated food plot in the five to seven-acre size range in the right location, deer will come to it from a distance of a mile or more. They may not come every day, but they will frequent the field on a regular basis throughout the winter. If you set it up right so that you approach the field from its south side, have the shooting house on its southern edge and choose to hunt it only when the wind is from the north (read cold), you will have a choice spot. So, the idea is to watch the papers, real estate listings, and local land office for small plots of land in rural areas ranging in size from ten to fifty acres and purchase these small acreages as they come available. Once owned, set about establishing a field well within its interior, being careful to pay attention to the details discussed above. In the last thirty years, I've seen land (for raw dirt, minus any timber) prices range from $175/acre to $2500/acre in rural areas near my home in Alabama. I've seen it below $200/acre twice in the last thirty years. And given our current economy and considering inflation-adjusted dollars, I suspect we will see those lows again. By saving your nickels, one can acquire true assets (i.e., grow timber) that will likely accrue some value (i.e., speculation) over time and provide some first-class hunting spots for your entire family. For example, consider that thirty acres at $500/acre comes to $15,000. Over time, this is within most hunters' reach. Some of these may even have a ravine or two that can be converted to a prime bass lake at minimal expense. Over a lifetime, it would be possible to accumulate a good many of these small acreages, all within easy driving distance of your home and all providing some really fine outdoor fun. Unlike big tracts, if you really got in a bind, these small acreages are pretty easy to liquidate for quick cash. But more importantly, you would like to have something to show for your lease money by the time you are ready to retire, not to mention a place to take your grandchildren

hunting and fishing.

Commercial Hunting Lodges

Most of my hunting success has been achieved on public land and private leased land. But there is another (and better) option in addition to those discussed above. As you by now realize, I have also spent a lot of time working with commercial hunting operations. In the late 1970s I joined West Alabama's Westervelt Lodge's (www.Westervelt.com) staff as an instructor for a series of bow hunting schools that spanned three decades. In the early 1980s, I began working with Bent Creek Lodge (www.BentCreekLodge.com) in Choctaw County, Alabama, to develop software they would use to manage their vast 45,000-acre hunting and fishing operations. In addition, we added a series of bow hunting schools (see www.BobSheppard.com) which continue to this day. In the late 1980s, I formed a not-for-profit educational foundation, called Progressive Medical Education, Inc. designed to allow physicians to acquire CME (continuing medical education) in a hunting and fishing environment. The meetings were hosted by the cream of the crop commercial hunting lodges across America like Bent Creek Lodge. During most of the 1980s, I was a member of OWAA (Outdoor Writers Association of America) and SEOPA (Southeastern Outdoor Press Association) and joined a group of outdoor writers, distributors, and manufacturers assembled to help manufacturers of hunting equipment, clothing, and related gear to gain recognition in the growing outdoor market. All these relationships paved the way for me to spend several weeks each winter at the premier commercial hunting lodges across the country. It was not as glittery as the Outdoor Channel because I worked on the business side of these operations in the background. But, I was there and enjoyed every moment of it. Granted, I didn't have to pay out of pocket for all this hard work, but it did allow me to get a good feel for what this kind of hunting really costs. Looking back, I can say without a moment's hesitation that if you visited these commercial lodges each year and spent the amount you would have spent going the home land leasing route, there is no doubt in my mind that at the end of thirty years, you would have spent less per trophy animal paying the price to hunt the best places in the country. I would venture further that you would have more and better trophy animals in your collection at the end going the commercial lodge route. As a side benefit, you will meet some of the finest people in the world. Individuals who frequent these places are generally successful folks who value their time. They are a pleasure to spend time with and are often knowledgeable across a vast range of subjects. Many of my most successful business decisions and investments were born of casual evenings at these fine lodges. There is one downside to this approach, however. You will weigh a lot more! The food at these places rivals a five-star hotel.

Reviewing The Data

Before reviewing the data, I should first set the stage for how and why we accumulated such data and give some explanation for what data we thought worthy of tracking. As I have mentioned elsewhere in this book, in the early years of my hunting, I had been pretty successful in taking a lot of whitetails. Twenty-five years of academic pursuits through grade school, college, medical school, and residency had left me with a tendency to approach most problems with a bit of an analytical bent. It was never enough for me to see that things happen. I always wanted to know why. I could see from those early years that whitetails had the tendency to come to large bean fields in the afternoon each day, and there, I could take them at will. But charging into pursuit with a stick and string changed things entirely. Suddenly, it was not good enough to know that they would come to a five hundred-acre bean field. To take one with a bow, I had to have some idea of when they would arrive, from what direction, and on what days would they likely come. And that said nothing of local weather conditions. I noticed that on any given day, my odds of taking one of these free-ranging mystics with a bow ran somewhere in the 5 percent range. That meant I had to hunt twenty afternoons for every successful hunt I would pull off. These statistics just simply drove me nuts. I longed for the day when I could improve those odds by ten fold. It was that single-minded determination that got me through medical school, and it would allow me to achieve a level of success few would ever see in the world of the whitetail. Given what I know about the weather's effect on whitetails, the weather service's ability to tell me what the next couple of days hold, having the advantage of carbon arrows, compound bows, pivotal sights, peep sights, mechanical releases, warm quiet clothing, climbing tree stands, and razor sharp broadheads has convinced me the American Indians likely ate relatively little venison. Granted, they had no seasons, bag limits, nor jobs to attend. I simply wanted to be able to know when to go to the woods, where in those woods to set up, and to have the skill to take any animal that might wander within range. That I have accomplished. Allow me to select the conditions we're about to discuss, and I can enjoy better than 90 percent odds of returning to the lodge with a deer taken with a bow and arrow! Is this not information you would like to know?

Based upon my own prior hunting experience, talking with other experienced hunters, and this tempered by what I had read, I was curious just what effect several weather factors might have on the statistical odds of seeing, and ultimately taking a whitetail, particularly with a bow. As a result, we have meticulously catalogued data from NOAA (National Oceanic & Atmospheric Administration) on wind direction, wind velocity, temperature, change in temperature, barometric pressure, change in barometric pressure, cloud cover, precipitation, quantity of precipitation, moon phase, moonrise time, and moonset time. These data were merged daily with each individual hunter's experience in the woods at Bent Creek Lodge, one of America's premier commercial hunting operations. Bent Creek owns and/or manages more than 45,000 acres of prime whitetail habitat in the Black Belt region of central Alabama. They have been managing this whitetail herd for more than thirty years. This fact combined with the weather data set the stage for us to study whitetail habits in a way never before approached. Every morning and every afternoon, we would send a couple of dozen hunters to the woods and then catalog what they saw, what they killed, and under what weather conditions they hunted. Key points captured for each morning hunt and each afternoon hunt include the number of deer sighted, number of does sighted, number of bucks sighted, type of bucks sighted, number of deer taken, number of does taken, and number of bucks taken. Each deer was weighed, had its jawbone pulled for aging, its antlers measured, and its general health assessed. Each of the above mentioned pieces of weather data were then merged with the morning and afternoon deer sighting and kill data. This creates an enormous database of hunter experience spanning more than a decade encompassing more than 35,000 "hunter days." Just imagine for a moment if you could go hunting 35,000 times and then look back at your experience through a grid that allowed you to realize how many deer you saw under a variety of weather conditions! You would soon get a very clear idea of when to hunt and when to do something else.

In the early years of this data collection, we utilized what is commonly referred to as "univariate analysis," meaning we were analyzing one variable at a time, but with little control over what other factors might be having on the variable we were trying to assess. Let me illustrate what I mean with an example. Based upon my own experience, I had the preconceived idea that the hunting would not be as good on a day following a night of full moon. In other words, if the moon phase was "bright" or within a day or two of being a full moon, but also the moonrise time was in the late afternoon/evening hours (meaning the bright phase of the moon would be up during the nighttime hours), then I had concluded the hunting would be suboptimal the following day. Having drawn this conclusion, I had even surmised why the hunting might not be as good the next day. It simply made sense to me that if these deer had more light by which to feed through the night hours, then indeed they would. When I reviewed the first couple of years of data, they indeed revealed there was nearly a fourfold reduction in deer sightings during the days hunted following full moons. My many years of experience and observation were confirmed. Or so I thought! Two more years passed, and I continued to study the data. Then, to my chagrin, I realized the trend had almost reversed during the third and fourth years of data collection. What was going on here? Why did my theory fall apart?

The good news is that as the data set grew, we were able to approach the problem with a more powerful statistical tool called "multivariate analysis." In this situation, we are able to hold a range of related variables constant, while assessing the statistical effect a single variable has on a second variable. For example, given all other variables resting within the same range (barometric pressure, cloud cover, moon phase, wind velocity, etc.), what would be the statistical odds of seeing a deer if the temperature were between 55 and 75 degrees compared to the same data but with the temperature between 25 and 45 degrees? Remember that we even have the data matched to actual deer kills, not just deer sightings (though, not surprisingly, kills track sighting just as you would expect). That means that we can look at the statistical odds of killing a male deer that is four and a half years old and, for all other variables being similar, but the temperature between 25 and 35 degrees. This can then be compared to the same dataset but with a temperature range of 65 to 75 degrees. The results are quite staggering.

Oh! The moon. That's right; you wanted to know what was stifling the deer sightings if it wasn't the full moon. As we worked our way through the data, a single factor emerged as the major force driving daytime deer sightings...the temperature. It turns out that during those first two seasons, by chance, unseasonably warm weather had coincided with the days following those bright moonlit nights. However, again by chance, during the moonlit nights of the third and fourth seasons, the weather was relatively cold, and deer sightings during the days following soared. Ensuing years revealed a range between these two extremes, but one factor shined supreme, and it was not the moon—no pun intended. Regardless of the moon phase, the cooler the weather the more deer the hunters sighted. The warmer the weather, the fewer deer hunters sighted.

Barometric Pressure

At first, I thought barometric pressure was going to rival the temperature as a factor influencing deer movement, but it turns out that as an independent variable, it has little, if any effect on the whitetail's daytime movement. It does, however, have the tendency to change in inverse proportions to temperature. As a result, it would appear to the casual observer, paying attention to it, to be driving deer movement. Meaning that when the temperature drops down, the mercury tends to rise as a rough approximation. As long as this relationship holds, you will see deer movement track barometric pressure ...the higher the pressure, the better the hunting. However, there are times when the barometer does not track the temperature well, and it is during these times that it becomes clear that the temperature is the driving force to their daytime movement and not the barometric pressure.

Temperature

After nearly twenty years of dissecting these data, there is absolutely no question that temperature reigns supreme as the weather factor that drives daytime whitetail movement. It will override rain, clouds, wind, and yes, even the rut. As you have discerned from this book about whitetails, if the weather is warm, I simply do not hunt. In Alabama, it makes that much of a difference. I've hunted in Texas a little, and it is actually possible to see good deer there in warm weather. But even there, let the temperature drop thirty degrees, and the number and quality of animals soar. Now, do hunters take deer, even good ones, during spells of warm weather? Of course they do. But I don't play that game. That kind of hunting is supported by the same nonsense upon which the lottery is based. When you plop down your money against the lottery systems of the world, you will be consistently defeated. And the more you play, the more consistently you will be defeated! Why do people do such foolish things? It's like the old adage from Albert Einstein that suggested, "Insanity is defined as doing the same thing over and over, but continuing to expect a different result." Once I realized what my odds of taking a deer in unseasonably warm weather really was, I simply stopped doing the same stupid thing over and over, expecting a different result.

The first lecture I present each year in my bow hunting schools (see www.BobSheppard.com and follow the hunting links) begins with a slide presentation graphically representing a basic set of premises that include a hunter going to the woods under a defined set of conditions. The story begins with an inexperienced hunter wandering aimlessly into a hundred-acre woodlot and there climbing a tree. His odds of taking a whitetail run somewhere in the 1 percent range, likely less. During the first few years I hunted, I longed for the day when I could take a deer on half my hunts. In other words, each time I would go to the woods and hunt for say, five hours, I strived to achieve a 50 percent kill rate even though I suspected there was no way to approach such odds with a bow. Today, more than thirty years later, allow me the luxury of choosing the variables around which I will hunt, and I can approach an odds ratio of better than nine to one that I will come home with a whitetail on my truck, every day. In recent years, I had a young man named Rill Banks attend one of our bow hunting schools. Rill would later become a very good friend and hunting companion. Turned out, he lived in Tuscaloosa, near my home. After the hunting season, he invited me to speak at a church fellowship meeting designed to get kids together with their parents to enjoy the outdoors. As he was introducing me to the large gathering, he made a statement that brought this concept home. He said, "When you finish hearing what Dr. Sheppard has to say about deer hunting, you will be impressed with how much he understands about these incredible animals. However, even after I heard his lecture and saw the amazing five-foot high pile of antlers from deer he has taken, that was not what impressed me the most. As we gathered our gear to go to the woods the first afternoon, he said, 'I will return to the lodge with a deer this evening and so should you.' For him to stand there before a group of experienced hunters and virtually guarantee that he would return with a deer seemed almost foolish. That evening, he indeed returned, not just with a deer, but with a nice eight-point and a doe."

That first afternoon of the bow school had presented us with near ideal conditions, and it wasn't that I was trying to be cocky. I just knew that the conditions were near perfect. And when the conditions are near perfect, I had a lot of confidence in what was likely going to happen. I had been in my stand about twenty minutes when the eight-point appeared from a cane-choked swamp. He was eating acorns from a white oak near the edge of the swamp when I let go of the arrow. He bounced about five yards, stood there in the cane for a few seconds, then slumped to the ground. An hour later, two does appeared from the same thicket. I took the oldest one and began my trek back to retrieve my Rokon™. I would not visit that spot again until the following season. Not frequenting the spot, knowing how and when to take the shot, then hunting it only under near perfect weather conditions coalesced to raise my odds of success to near perfection. I was simply playing out what our data had confirmed would happen across thousands of hunts.

Now, let's talk in a bit more detail about the temperature. If cooler weather is good, is bitter cold even better? Well, the answer is, "Probably." If you are hunting in Alabama in mid-October and the temperature is running in the eighties, but suddenly drops into the sixties, you will see a noticeable rise in daytime deer activity. If it should drop from the eighties into the forties, you will notice a huge surge in daytime activity. In January, when the cooler temperatures tend to run in the low twenties in our area, a day in the forties is likely to see relatively little daytime whitetail movement. So, in a sense, the effect the temperature has on daytime deer movement is relative. It is relative to the time of year, but also to the absolute temperature. Cold weather will overcome a lot of other hunter sins, but why force the issue. Hunt when the conditions are nearing perfection...cold, clear, windy weather in a location set up for a north wind and seldom visited. Over a lifetime of hunting, the results will be the envy of any wanting hunter.

By the way, many hunters stunned by the stack of trophies I've taken over the last thirty-five years always come back with an obvious question. "Why haven't you mounted these trophies? You have animals here scoring in the 150s and 160s!" To this I really just don't have a good answer. With each animal taken, I just kept thinking I would kill a bigger one. I finally reached a point where the cumulative effect of all the antlers together was more impressive than covering most of the walls in my home with them would have been...and a lot less expensive. At today's prices, just to mount the larger ones would set one back well over $35,000!

Wind

I must confess that I held to a lot of misconceptions about what effect weather had on daytime deer movement when I first started hunting. For example, I thought that a near calm wind would be particularly good if the weather was cold. That turned out not to be the case. As whitetails begin to emerge from their daytime sanctuaries, they are incredibly cautious. The older they are, the more cautious they become. They have spent the day in the confines of a secure and safe environment. When there is little to no wind stirring the foliage, a whitetail tends to take a few steps and then listen for several minutes from a single position to every little noise. Whereas, when the wind is moving the foliage enough to make some noise, they will tend to tarry for a much shorter time in a single spot. As a result, they tend to cover more ground as the wind picks up. During the bow season, I much prefer a cool day with a ten to fifteen mile per hour wind over a more calm day with the same temperature. But I had another very wrong misconception. I thought that the sighting curve would flatten out as the wind velocity moved much past the fifteen mile per hour range. However, I would learn from our data collection efforts that deer sightings form a nearly linear relationship to wind velocity. In other words, the harder the wind blows, the more deer are sighted. This came as a surprise to me, and even with the data staring at me, I doubted it for several years. As I tried to play it out, I began to realize why most of us had drawn the conclusion that really windy, cold weather was not good hunting. It had nothing to do with the deer. It had to do with the fact that when the temperature is in the twenties or colder, and the wind in the twenty to thirty mile per range, we, as hunters, simply cannot carry enough clothes to the woods to remain comfortable in Alabama. As a result, we don't stay in the tree for long under these conditions. That's why we don't see the deer. They are moving under these conditions. We just can't tolerate the conditions well enough to remain aloft.

Some fifteen years ago, I was guiding an outdoor writer from Sports Afield at a commercial hunting lodge in Alabama. I don't want to embarrass the gent, so I won't divulge his name. But if I did, you would know it instantly. Even for January, the weather was really cold. When we got out of the truck the first morning, I noticed that he had on a single layer of modest fleece. I suggested that I thought he might be a shade underdressed for this kind of weather. He smiled and said assuringly, "Dr. Sheppard, I hunt South Dakota regularly in weather well below zero in these clothes. I can handle this just fine." A little surprised, I countered, "Well, sir, this is not South Dakota, and you are about to learn a hard lesson about the South." With that, we were off to the woods. I walked him about half a mile to a narrow bottleneck between two hardwood shears near a wet swamp on the river. I showed him which tree to climb, from which direction the deer would likely emerge, and which way to face his stand. A few hours later, clad with every piece of clothing I owned, I just couldn't take the cold any longer. I climbed down and made my way to his stand site. As I walked up to the tree, in spite of my sounding like an elephant in the frozen leaves, he didn't acknowledge my approach. I stood there for a moment looking up at him. Still, he didn't move. Finally, I became a little worried and yanked on the rope he had used to pull his bow up. Slowly, he leaned and gazed down at me. I was relieved and light heartedly asked, "Well, did you see anything?" It's simply not possible to put into print what he said. First, it was pretty coarse, and second, I don't think I could convey the look on his face. He did indicate that a really nice eight-point had passed twelve yards to the left of his stand. He was so cold, he wasn't able to get to a standing position for several seconds, but even when he finally did, he couldn't draw his bow. The buck walked away never knowing he was there. "Welcome to Alabama," I offered through a frozen smile.

So much for wind velocity. What about wind direction? Well, it might surprise you to find that our data indicated that wind direction has no independent effect on daytime deer sightings. On first blush this might seem pretty counter too much of what I have said, but actually it is not.

Remember the effect of barometric pressure. When the barometer is high, it is usually cooler. Well, the same is true for the wind. When the wind is blowing from the north, the weather tends to be cooler. So, once again, when we hold all the other variables within a pretty tight range and focus on wind direction's effect on deer sightings, the wind direction has no independent effect on the statistical odds of seeing deer in the daylight hours. Once again, it is the temperature that is driving the daytime movement. The wind and barometric pressure are simply along for the ride. But just remember what I said in other chapters. I don't even set up a spot to hunt with a south wind, but the underlying reason is still the temperature so often associated with that south wind that makes the difference. If you had a day in the winter with a south wind when the temperature was falling (a rare, but possible scenario), then you might well have a good day to hunt. I wouldn't hold my breath. Let's place our money on the horse that won most of the other races.

Rain

It just made sense to me given that whitetails are nocturnal animals, that they would prefer cloudy/rainy conditions because it more closely fit their nocturnal nature. Once again, I could not have been further from the truth. Our data clearly reveal that, given all other conditions being similar, you will see more deer on clear days than cloudy ones, and more deer on cloudy days than rainy ones. I have taken some nice deer in cold rainy weather. I have taken nothing in warm rainy weather. Worried about your feather fletch getting wet? Don't. Stay at the camp house. You'll take just about as many deer there under such conditions!

I have now discussed three variables, all of which have a distinct and independent effect on the statistical odds of a hunter seeing a whitetail during the daytime hours ...temperature, wind velocity, and cloud cover. But how do they stack up against each other? If I should weigh these factors on a scale from one to ten, I would give temperature a ten. It is, hands down, the primary factor that drives daytime herd movement of the whitetail. Wind velocity is a close second. I would give it a seven out of ten on the scale. Cloud cover, particularly clear weather, I would give a five out of ten. Again, I'm stating that a cold, windy, clear day represents the absolute prime weather conditions for pursuing and taking a whitetail with any weapon, but particularly a bow and arrow. The older the animal you are pursuing, the more important these factors become. Just bear in mind that even under near perfect conditions, more than ninety percent of a given herd will remain within the confines of a sanctuary during daylight hours. We, as hunters, are hunting a mere 10 percent of the local herd. That 10 percent is the only part of the herd that moves outside their safety zone in daylight hours. When conditions are poor, that percentage drops to less than 1 percent. Again, why fight the odds when they are stacked so against us?

Fronts

Since at all times, these weather conditions tend to come as mixtures, I think it is helpful to consider them as such. We refer to a weather front as a typical pattern of change that we see in winter weather. I had read many times that deer had a tendency to feed in advance of impending harsh changes in weather. That is true for many fish species. But again, nothing could have been farther from the truth for the whitetail. Deer do not tend to move well ahead of a front. As an example, let's say it is warm and rains most of the day and into the evening hours. By 8:00 or 9:00 p.m., the wind begins to shift from the south around to the southwest and then to the west. The temperature begins to drop and as the wind blows harder and shifts to the northwest, morning emerges with the previous day's rain frozen, the wind howling, and the temperature having dropped thirty degrees or more. It then remains

186

cold for several days, but slowly warms over five to seven days, then repeats the cycle. That is a typical front cycle in west Alabama where I live and hunt. Let's grade daytime deer movement on each of those seven days using the scale from one to ten, one being worst and ten being the best hunting conditions. The warm, rainy day with a south wind would rate a zero. I would never go to the woods on a day like this. However, the following bitter cold, windy, clear day would rate a ten. The second day with a modest wind still blowing following the front would rate an eight. The third day would rate a five. The fourth day would rate a three and so on until warm, cloudy, rainy weather repeats the cycle. On occasion, it will still be raining that second morning, but cold and windy. Instead of a ten, I would rate such a day a six or perhaps a seven. In other words, the rain deteriorates the odds of taking a deer considerably in spite of the excellent cold, windy conditions. Except when I'm at the bow schools (I hunt most any conditions then to keep morale up.), I tend to hunt on my own leases only when conditions are in the seven to ten range.

Moon Phase

Perhaps more has been written about the moon's effect on game activity than any other weather factor. Yet, we have found it to be a non event.

187

There is no question about the moon's effect on many fish species with respect to spawning, but mammals, I think, are a very different story. In fact, as I was reviewing these data, I would have not been at all surprised to have found the moon phase exerting a significant effect. When I was a medicine resident, we often mused that it seemed like people did the craziest things near a full moon. We would draw straws to see who had to work on full moon nights because it seemed the emergency rooms would be full of people with acute psychosis, suicide attempts, nervous breakdowns, gunshot wounds, knife stabbings, and on and on. However, I suspect this is just our powers of reason running the ox into the ditch. If you have cold, clear, windy weather...forget the moon! Unless, of course, you wish to howl at it now and again.

Equipment of Choice

This is certain to be controversial, but it is fun to talk about. In fact, I would dare say that more than half of what most hunters chat about in the camp is focused around their equipment. With few exceptions, I will make no friends of the sporting goods manufacturers because as you will see, I am not picky in general about brands. I am bent upon supreme performance, however. That fact, of itself, sometimes drives one to specific brands, or worse, to custom construction and design.

Guns

Not only have thousands of articles, but scores of books have been written about the ideal whitetail gun. I'll break this section down into two parts, (1) first the gun itself and (2) then the cartridge it handles.

My deer hunting began with a Browning BLR chambered in the .308 cartridge. It was a short, light, and handy carbine typical of Browning's good quality. However, accurate, it was not. One could achieve a good solid six-inch group at 100 yards with some coaxing. That was, of course, with factory bullets and an inexpensive scope. It didn't take me long to figure out that this combo was not adequate for the large bean fields. My wife gave me a really nice bolt action Colt-Sauer™ chambered in 30–06 caliber for Christmas more than thirty years ago, and this sweet shooter became the staple of my long-range hunting for many years to come.

Just before I completed my residency in internal medicine in the late 1970s, this same sterling wife saved her milk and egg money to fund the adventure of my dreams. I had always wanted a custom built rifle. Is there any wonder I have clung to this jewel of a woman for more than thirty-five years! I searched for the better part of a year just for an ideal piece of wood. This turned out to be a piece of exhibition grade myrtle. This incredibly beautiful piece of nature was sent to the custom gun maker, Harry Lawson in Tucson, Arizona, who crafted it into a beautiful little carbine called the Cochise Thumbhole™. It was ported and chambered for the venerable .308 cartridge. It became the chosen weapon for my "woods hunting" for the next twenty-five years, and I have taken hundreds of whitetails with it. I continue to hunt with it today.

In the chapter on advanced hunting tactics, I covered the story of my fourth weapon, the 300 Remington Ultra Mag™ and will not recount that again here. I won't spend a lot of time on the details of the history of these calibers and guns, but rather I simply outline the logic behind the development of each. I needed a weapon that would allow me to shoot at least 200 yards, and the 30–06 Sauer stepped up to the plate quite nicely. It had moderate recoil weighing in at about nine pounds sporting a simple but functional walnut stock, rosewood forepiece, and glossy sporter barrel. I gradually worked up some really hot handloads well outside the reloading manual's upper limits that were capable of three-quarter inch groups at 100 yards. I never had a case separation, flattened primer, nor split case from it, though I'll admit to throwing the cases away after only five or six reloadings. I've had far more case failures with my .308 loaded very moderately though, again, I tend to go to about twenty reloadings on these, and this likely accounts for the higher frequency of case failures. I start with LC Match cases in the .308 and factory cases for the 30–06. The 300 RUM is based on the .404 Jeffery elephant cartridge, but I never fire formed my own cases. I just used Remington's factory cases and have never had a case failure. The 300 RUM gave me the ultimate weapon to shoot accurately to 400 yards and beyond. The .308 Lawson™ gave me a light, accurate, and handy gun for use in a tree stand. And everytime I look down at that exquisite piece of myrtle, my mind drifts to this wonderful woman God has given me.

Cartridges and Bullets

My choice of bullets is again a result of the wide range of options available through hand loading. I generally use 150 grain Nosler Partitions™ in my .308. They always open, regardless of the muzzle velocity. I use 165 grain Nosler Ballistic Tips™ for the 300 RUM. The 3500 fps muzzle velocity leaves the sleek bullet traveling well beyond my .308's muzzle velocity even after the 300 goes past the quarter-mile mark!

Because I hunt in a variety of weather conditions, I have always favored free-floated barrels as opposed to the center pointed approach to bedding. The latter are generally more precise in terms of accuracy, but the former are more forgiving (consistent) in a wide range of weather conditions. All these guns were either custom built in the first place, as in the example of the Lawson™ .308, or customized by a good gunsmith to squeeze out their best accuracy potential. The adjustments I refer to are simple and relatively inexpensive adjustments (like squaring the bolt face, smoothing the locking lugs, adjusting the trigger and working on the bedding) and there are many gunsmiths who can help with your gun. If you don't know anyone and need work on an existing gun, I recommend Jim McCullough's group at 494 Seymore Road, Selma, Alabama 36701 (334–875–6443). If you want a custom fit that will outshoot anything on the earth, contact Kenny Jarrett at www.jarrettrifles.com. His rifles are pricey, but when you miss with a Jarrett rifle, you are the problem. If you wonder how I know, I shoot a Jarrett™ .223 bolt and hunt with Kenny each summer sniping prairie dogs in Wyoming. I've taken these coffee cup-sized varmints at more than half a mile with the .223! Four hundred-yard shots are a matter of squeezing the trigger. But we digress. Back to whitetail basics. What alterations to your off the shelf rifle are necessary? I would leave this to the gunsmith's suggestions, but it has been my experience that how the barrel is fastened to the action is a key weak point in accuracy. This will likely need to be addressed. Second, the trigger is a key focal point. It should be relatively light. My deer rifles run about thirty to forty ounces, and my Jarrett .223 is half that. They have absolutely no creep and no overtravel. A good trigger will take a lot of the missing out of poor form and a speedy heart.

Scopes

I am not picky about scopes, but currently have Leopold on all my guns including the Jarrett. Oddly enough the only scope failure I have ever experienced was a very pricey Zeiss™ I had originally on the custom Lawson™ .308. To their credit, Zeiss™ fixed it without charge, but I have not used it since. I have never had a Leopold fail, but there are so many good optics on the market, I would just leave this decision to your discretion with the exception of one caveat. I would not spend less than the cost of the rifle (except for a Jarrett™, of course) on the scope/mount combination. This is a crucial part of consistent accuracy and reliability. The base and rings are just as important as the optics. For woods hunting, I like the 3x9 variable range scopes and the 4x12 variable range scopes for long range shooting. Both utilize the standard 4-Plex style reticle. Of course, long-range deer shooting is not varmint hunting. My Jarrett .223 sports a Leopold 6x24 with a very fine reticle and a turret customized to a prime hand reload.

Reloading

One can eliminate a lot of sins inherent to a rifle by utilizing good basic reloading. You will never save a penny reloading rifle cartridges, but if you want custom rounds that will be reliable (never had a failure in thirty years of handloading) and dramatically enhance the accuracy of your rifle, I would definitely give it a try. The equipment to get started is cheap (less than $200), lasts a lifetime, and is simple to learn. There are a host of free references on the Internet to help you get started. The idea is to start with a load toward the middle of a loading manual's range for a given bullet/powder combination, and work your way up about half a grain at a time, testing each load for accuracy and signs of high pressures before advancing to the next higher powder charge. Somewhere along that exercise, you will likely stumble upon a case/primer/bullet/powder combination that your particular rifle will really like. From that day forward, you just assemble a few of those favorite loads for each season, and you are off to the races.

Rifle	308	ARS Lawson	
Bullet	150	Grains	Nosler BT Solid Base
Powder	45	Grains	IMR 4064
Case	Federal		
Primer	CCI 200		
Date Shot	6/1/1984		
Group Measurement	0.9	Inches	
# of Shots	3		
Temperature	70 to 80 Degrees		
Cartrige Length	2.780	Inches	
Muzzel Velocity		FPS	
Source of Load			
General Information	Clear, Moderate, & Relatively Calm		

Rifle	308	ARS Lawson	
Bullet	150	Grains	Nosler BT Solid Base
Powder	46	Grains	IMR 4064
Case	Federal		
Primer	CCI 200		
Date Shot	11/30/2002		
Group Measurement	1.3	Inches	
# of Shots	3		
Temperature	70 to 80 Degrees		
Cartrige Length	2.780	Inches	
Muzzel Velocity		FPS	
Source of Load			
General Information	Clear, Moderate, & Relatively Calm		

I would mention one last factor to consider with your centerfire rifle. Keep it sighted in. I usually load some twenty to thirty rounds at the beginning of each season and about once per week, I shoot my gun one round at a 200-yard target. As long as that single shot is where I want it, I'm okay. You don't need three shot groups for this kind of frequent checking of your sights. Sometimes I will go years at a time with no change in the point of impact, then just about the time I think this exercise isn't necessary, I find it off by several inches for no apparent reason. It is likely that a big part of this frequent checking of my sights has more to do with my confidence when I pull the trigger at the moment of reckoning. If I shoot, I am nearly one hundred percent confident that I made a lethal shot. This is not to say that I never miss, but when I do, I do not stop until I find out why. This confidence in my ability to hit what I'm shooting at also gives me the confidence to just keep looking when I don't find the deer in short order, or when there is no blood trail to follow.

For a free copy of my reloading database program you can use to keep track of your favorite loads, go to my Website (www.BobSheppard.com or http://www.bobsheppard.com/BobSheppard.com/

and follow the download links to the Reloading Database.

A Personal Dose of Reality

Let me digress to relate an example of what I mean. Many years ago when I first started hot loading the 30–06, I had a shooting lane where the farthest shot was well beyond the 400-yard mark. One morning, I saw a heavy beamed nine-point step into the shooting lane at its far end ...about 445 yards away! I held the crosshair about one inch above the top of his back and tightened down on the trigger. Just as I was preparing my mind for the recoil, he started to walk. I was mentally sort of committed, and so I finished squeezing the trigger. I recovered from the recoil and was looking through the scope when he suddenly appeared in the shooting lane about 150 yards closer to me, but now facing the other way as though looking back to see what had happened. I lowered the crosshair to high on his chest and squeezed the trigger again. He hit the dirt like a sack of rocks. I walked down to the deer and found that about half of his tail was missing and the stub was actively bleeding. That meant the first shot had missed by nearly two feet! Perhaps most hunters under those circumstances might concede that such a miss is reasonable. But I wasn't buying it. I was absolutely certain I could not have missed by two feet. I had a solid sandbag rest, clear sight picture, no wind, no rain, no distractions, and as the second shot suggested and I later confirmed, my rifle was perfectly zeroed for the shot. The next evening, I was sitting at my reloading bench, still puzzled by the odd miss. Then, I got to thinking, Wonder how long it would take a bullet to go 400 yards at an average of about 2700 fps? The answer ...about half a second. Working through the math indicated that a deer walking a leisurely three miles per hour would cover just about two feet in half a second! In spite of doing my job very precisely, he had literally walked out of the path of the bullet due to the extended distance, except of course, were it not for that little white tail that engenders his namesake. I learned that lesson well. If he's moving, I don't shoot.

Binoculars

Good binoculars are absolutely crucial to successful whitetail hunting. My field and long-range binoculars are large glass 10x60 Swarovski™. The Swarovski's are more than thirty years old. My woods hunting glasses are Leopold Mesa™ 8x23 compacts. When I'm in a tree in the deep woods, I utilize the compact Leopold's. When I'm glassing a field in late evening, I use the big glass, lightgathering Swarovski's.

Range Finders

The only time I use a range finder is when I'm shooting prairie dogs. In the woods where I hunt, if I can see him, I can kill him. The long shooting lanes I have come to treasure don't allow enough time for range finding. Most often, there is barely enough time to check him out in the scope and pull the trigger.

Carrying Cases

Hunting near my home, I utilize a simple, soft, and inexpensive cloth zippered case. If you travel much, however, a good carrying case is really necessary. The airlines these days will go out of their way to destroy anything that resembles a gun case. The anti-hunting sentiment in America is becoming intense. My favorite is the virtually indestructible Storm™ case (http://www.militarycases.com/ StormCases.html). It is wonderful sport to stand at the big glass windows gazing onto the tarmac and watch the airline employees try to destroy a Storm™ rifle case. They can stomp it, kick it, toss it off the top of the baggage trailer, and run over it with the tarmac hauler, but all they get is a sore foot. If you have a fine piece of equipment, put it in a Storm™.

Bows and Related Gadgets

As I mentioned early on, I started with Bear™ bows because Fred Bear was the earliest sponsor of our bow hunting schools (www.BobSheppard.com and follow the hunting links to bow schools). Later, I acquired a custom Black Widow™ takedown recurve and took dozens of whitetails and several bears with it. In passing years, we worked with several manufacturers including Browning™, Hoyt™, and Mathews ™. To be honest, I could never really tell a lot of difference between brands nor models of compounds once you got past about the $300 cost range. I shot a Browning Mag Reflex™ for a long time and took dozens of deer with it. The same was true for a Mathews Feathermax™. However, I must confess a revelation with my last bow acquisition. The Mathews Drenalin™ is by my experience, in a class by itself. I have never shot a bow that is so simple, balanced, smooth, forgiving, and accurate. I am just rock solid confident that I can make the shot with it and confidence means a lot in hunting.

As I also indicated earlier, I am not much on gadgets for bows nor guns. Having said that, I have some unusual opinions concerning the gadgets I do use. Because of my years with the recurve, I was slow to accept overdraws, mechanical releases, peeps and sight pins. Hard headed as I am, though, reality did slowly sink in. At our bow hunting schools each fall, there are always a few traditional archers attending, and I was in their camp for a long time. Now, I am fond of saying early on,"The traditional hunter is the hunter who truly loves the hunt, but if you like venison, get yourself a good compound."

There is a four-part system of sighting when you are using a compound each of which is crucial to good accuracy. They are the
(1) sight pin, (2) peep, (3) arrow rest, and (4) the mechanical release. Let's take a look at the function of each. I used a lot of different kinds of arrow rests, but settled on the TM Hunter™ style rest for the longest period. But a couple of years ago, I finally switched to the Whisker Biscuit™ and just can't imagine why I waited so long. This rest is simple, functional, and reasonably accurate. Unless you are an experienced target shooter, just get one. You will not regret it. There are a host of different types of peeps, and here, I am not picky. I use the Surz-a-peep™ style peep that is contained within the fibers of the string. No rubber tubing is required to make it line up,

and it comes in a variety of sizes. I always buy the peep with the largest hole I can find. Your eye will find the center of the larger circle automatically and shooting at twilight is easier through the larger peep. I shoot a Scott™ mechanical release, but I think there are several other good ones on the market. The key is to make certain it has the exact same features as a good rifle trigger ...light clean break, no over-travel, and no creep. I like the type I hold in my hand rather than the more popular Velcro™ style. None of the above is likely surprising, but the sight pin is where I venture far from the crowds and do not intend to return.

First, I would never think of hunting with more than one sight pin. I have seen far too many deer missed because of the difficulty of settling on the right pin in the heat of the moment when it comes time to shoot. As a result, I went back to a single pin many years ago. The pendulum style sight gives one some improvement over a single fixed pin, but not by much. However, there is one very unusual pendulum style pin on the market called an ABC Pivotal Sight System™ (check it out at: http://www.abcpivotal.com). It has a camming pivotal action rather than the standard pin that swings in a half circle. In a nutshell, that means that raising your bow a given amount alters the pin's position very differently for deer that are farther away compared to those that are closer by. The result is that one can hold dead on out to about sixty yards with a single pin! This sight is a royal pain in the butt to set up correctly, but worth its weight in gold once a good setup is accomplished. I had trouble with its adjustments tending to bottom out in the sight frame on the newest version, and I never could convince the manufacturer that they have a problem. I had purchased several of the earlier versions and just went back to one of these on my Mathews Drenalin™ bow. The sight's inherent weak points in the woods are that you must move the position of the sight frame depending upon the height you climb to. If you always climb to about the same height (which few of us do), then it works fine. The adjustment for stand height is built into the frame of the sight and works fine, but you just have to remember to do it each time you climb to a different height. In addition, the sight will not shoot accurately in hilly terrain. It shoots downhill fine, but if you try to shoot uphill at all, it will cause you to shoot completely over the deer. But remember that in the area where I hunt, a ridge is any land that does not hold standing water after a rain. In spite of all the aforementioned difficulties with this sight, being able to draw with a single sight picture out to sixty yards is simply worth the trouble. I do hope the manufacturer will work out the problem with the new version's adjustment system.

I just don't think the quiver type is much of a big deal, so I won't dwell on it. I use one that removes from the bow, holds six arrows, and fastens to the tree using a screw in attachment.

I am also not picky about arrows, though I do like the durability of the carbon arrows. I use Carbon Express™, but Gold Tips™ and Easton™ make other good arrows as well. The key is to match their spine to your bow's draw weight, draw length combination. I use a simple three or four-inch three vane fletch (though I stuck with feather fletch as long as I shot a recurve). I generally start by looking at the chart recommendations in a bow shop, then work my way down in arrow spine until I get erratic flight. I then move back up one measure in spine stiffness from there and settle with that combination of bow weight/arrow spine.

I wrote an article about broadheads for Southern Outdoors many years ago that was really controversial. I set up a study in which I shot fifty some odd types and brands of broadheads under very controlled conditions into several types of medium including foam, heavy plywood, meat, and meat with bone. I then cataloged each head's performance when hitting each of these types of medium. I got hate mail for months following the article's publication. It seems that none of the heads really performed well in most of the test results. The problem with this study (which I also stated in the article) was that all this stuff about head performance failed to translate into putting the deer on the ground, the prime objective of any good broadhead. Fortunately, most any broadhead will perform this function just fine. I'll admit that I like the three blade, cutting leading edge broadhead (meaning it cuts from the point all the way down to the ends of the blades). When I find one I like, I stick with it. I often take several dozen deer during a season, and shooting the mechanical heads would be a really expensive proposition. In addition, I'm not convinced they do any better job of putting the animal down quickly. So I stick with simple, inexpensive, three-blade broadheads. The most important characteristics of the arrow/broadhead combo is that they fly straight and that they pass completely through the animal upon impact. If the arrow remains within the deer (as is often the case with mechanical heads), the deer is two counties away when he finally stops running. More than half the deer I kill with a bow fall within sight of where I'm sitting. I like that. It's a comforting feeling to sit there the rest of the afternoon waiting on a second deer, but knowing success is only a few yards away.

Clothing and Camouflage

One afternoon several years ago, I was addressing a group of bow hunters at a prominent commercial hunting lodge who was hosting one of our bow hunting schools, when one of the guests popped the question, "What is your favorite camo pattern?"

I responded, "Well, to be honest, I just don't think it makes any difference. There are several really good ones on the market these days, like Mossy Oak™, Realtree™, and others, but I would not hesitate to hunt in blue jeans and a T-shirt." The young man had already painted his face a nice camo pattern for the afternoon hunt and really took offense to my suggestion. It just happened that the lodge had a camera crew present shooting some footage for an upcoming TV series. So, I countered with, "I tell you what. How about you go with me this afternoon, and we'll have the camera crew go as well. I'll hunt in blue jeans and a light-colored fleece jacket. No face paint. No gloves. No camo. You judge whether it makes a difference."

The other guests quickly chimed in and began to tease both of us, wagering amongst themselves who would emerge vindicated. The weather was turning cool, and I felt pretty certain I could get us set up in a position to get a shot. And if I did, I knew what was going to happen. I'd been there too many times before. He bit on my offer, and buzzed on about how this was going to be fun to watch.

I walked the crew about three-quarters of a mile into a fairly thick area of cane near the point of a slough bordering a big wet swamp. We sounded like a herd of elephants, and I'll admit that by the time I got us all up a tree, I was thinking I had probably run my mouth off one time too many. A couple of hours passed uneventfully, then I motioned to the cameraman. A big doe was entering the water on the far side of the slough. She slowly sloshed across the shallow end, walked about thirty yards up the gentle slope, and stopped only a few steps to my right. I stood perfectly still, but was perched only about twelve feet off the ground. The cameraman was above me and off to my left. Then she looked up at me, bobbed her head a couple of times, and dropped her left front foot hard against the ground.

The young fellow was sitting in a gum tree immediately to my left. He whispered, "Told you!"

I never broke the intent gaze locked onto her eyes, but countered without moving, "Just sit still. She doesn't yet know that she is dead!" She took about five quick steps forward with her head now behind a heavy walnut stump from a downfall. I eased my bow to full draw, settled the pin on her chest, and released. She bounced about fifteen yards, stopped looking back a few seconds, then wobbled and fell over.

My buddy said, "I can't believe such luck."

I countered, "I told you she didn't yet know that she was dead."

About thirty minutes later, I motioned to the cameraman down the slough almost behind us. A broad-based six-point was slowly making his way toward us through some cane. I stood, pivoted in the tree to face that direction and motioned for my buddy and the cameraman to make their position adjustments while he was hidden in the cane. When he was about twenty-five yards in front of me, he looked up at the cameraman.

I said, "Steady, don't move, don't move. Just hold perfectly still. He too does not yet know that he is dead." He cleared the cane about fifteen yards to my right, stood for a good minute then dropped his head and took a step forward. As he moved forward, his head and chest disappeared behind a holly bush. I eased my bow to full draw. Again, he stood for a long time. I was glad I was holding only a few of my bow's fifty pounds of draw weight. Finally, he took two more steps, and his head and chest cleared the bush. I settled the pin, held it there for several seconds more, then released. He jumped about five yards forward, wheeled around, and lunged toward the slough. At the water's edge, he hesitated, looking across the water, then slumped to the ground, kicked a couple of times, then lay still for a long time. By this point, I had a second arrow in my right hand, my bow still upright and pointed in his direction. I eased both down, settled to my seat and swiveled slowly to the cameraman and gave him the thumbs up. That night at the lodge, I didn't have to say a word. My young friend told it all ...again and again.

To be honest, I do use camo clothing, but not because of the

camo pattern, but rather because of the clothing design and material. Fleece has become a hunting staple. It is soft, quiet, comfortable, durable, and available in a host of patterns and styles. I just love it. And I think the popular patterns produced by Mossy Oak™, Realtree™, and others are beautiful and fitting clad for a hunting camp. It is simply part of the mystique of the hunting experience. I like it and I wear it...even though I don't need it.

Containing your emotions and not allowing them to cause you to move at the wrong instant is the key to success in those final few seconds. Don't worry about face paint and bare hands. If you need head and face cover and/or gloves to avoid being cold, no problem, wear them. When a whitetail looks up into my bare face and fails to see danger, it's a mistake he won't suffer to regret.

Boots

I have always liked Lacrosse™ boots, but a few years ago stumbled upon one I like even better, the Fieldblazer™ by Muck Boot™ (www.MuckBoots.com). They are much lighter and easier to get on and off but otherwise about the same as the Lacrosse™ varieties.

Tree Stands

This is another area where I wander pretty far from the crowd. My initial experience with tree stands was with the Baker™ brand of climbing stands. They probably should have aptly been named Baker™ falling stands, because they had a really bad tendency to just drop from underneath you. In fact, I understand they since have disappeared from the market because of liability issues. After a short exposure to these, I changed to the Loc-On™ style stand, but didn't stay with them long either. I just couldn't get comfortable. The array of climbing stands that since flooded the market are far safer, but all are bulky and heavy, a serious problem for a hunter as mobile as I tend to be. The whole experience remains a major compromise in maneuverability and comfort. Then a longtime friend of mine, Craig Thornton, came to me one day and said, "I'd like for you to just try this and tell me what you think." He had designed a most unusual approach to balancing oneself aloft. A guy named Jeff Anderson back in the 1960s had designed and patented a weblike stand fashioned after a window painter's seat (the Anderson Tree Sling™). Craig had taken this basic design in a very different direction and provided a framework around which the nylon webbing was fashioned. He had departed tremendously from Anderson's design approach and solved the two basic features that made the Anderson Tree Sling so uncomfortable: (1) the angle from the tree and (2) the fact that the webbing squeezed your butt like a Chinese cinch knot. The webbing was really strong and feather light. I can remember to this day the gum tree I sat in that first morning. I climbed up about daybreak, and at noon, I just kept sitting there thinking, I can't believe this thing! I am still comfortable. Craig made several improvements in its design, and went on to produce the stand commercially for a while under the trade name Saf-T-Rak™, but the stand never became popular. The difficulty of climbing the tree using screw-in or rope-on steps was difficult for most hunters, and there was something about the complexity of the rope/webbing combination that just seemed to confuse most hunters. I thought, So be it. It was the way to go as far as I was concerned, and I have continued to use his stand to this day, some thirty years later. It allows me to sit comfortably for hours, stand, swivel 360 degrees, shoot from any angle, and then sit again making no sudden movements, no noise, and all the while attached to the tree in two places, all the while encased within a web of safety. Should I go to sleep, it matters not. The stand's design holds the hunter upright in place even if he should become suddenly unconscious. Just remember, that climbing, like flying, is a dangerous venture. One can do it all perfectly for years, but make one mistake, and it can cost his life. I realize this thing can fail me, but I believe it to be the safest, most comfortable, and versatile stands in existence.

Every year at our bow schools, hunters want to know what kind of stand I hunt from, and I generally say, "Well, just a homemade stand," and try to drop it at that. At a recent school at Bent Creek Lodge in Alabama, one of our hunters, a really inquisitive general surgeon from Mississippi named Joe Bumgardner, just wouldn't take "no" for an answer. I finally gave in and went outside and showed him my stand. He immediately said, "I've seen this before." He described a very similar stand called the Guido's Web™ (http://www.guidosoutdoors.com)

designed and marketed by Butch Palasini from Mississippi. I later acquired one of Palasini's stands, and found it to be strikingly similar to the stand I had been using for nearly thirty years. Although I still favor my original homemade version, Butch has made some really interesting innovations to the basic idea of the window seat design. I'm interested in talking with him about this in more detail. With a couple of pretty minor changes, I might could be convinced to switch.

Climbing the tree is probably the part of hunting aloft that has baffled most hunters. The popularity of the climbing tree stand remains as a legacy to its difficulty in spite of its safety record. To climb, I use the old traditional screw-in steps for two reasons; (1) my stand weighs in at just over six pounds, and (2) the climbing stands are noisy, bulky, and weigh a ton. The steps are slow, but make no noise and allow one to easily slip up the tree completely undetected even with a whitetail lying down just a few yards away. The most important piece of information to know about my steps is in how I use them. I use a step starter to start and to finish screwing the steps into the tree. This simple little gadget allows one to nearly effortlessly start the step, but far more important than that, allows one to screw the step in just as effortlessly. Without it, I'd be looking for some other way up the tree, for sure. For the record, the E-Z Climb™

(http://www.escreamingeagle.com/ez-climb-
step.htm) steps comprise the simplest design and
allow the step starter to perfectly align for easily
placing the step using the step starter. The starter
is simple to build yourself. The handle is made
from an eight to ten-inch piece of PVC pipe.The
step is inserted into one end of the PVC handle.
A piece of bungee is looped around the screw to
keep it from folding when being inserted into the
tree. This simple combination makes ascending
the tree with lightweight, inexpensive steps a
cinch.

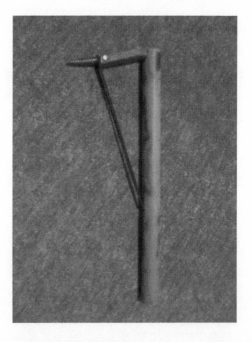

Simple step starter to help place screw-in steps into tree

Transportation and Cargo Racks

Transportation, once I arrive at my favorite hunting spot, has never been much of an issue for me. I bought an ATV many years ago but it sat under a shed until the tires cracked and broke open. The idea of roaring into my hunting area announcing my presence to the world was just never very appealing. Then on a trip into northwestern Quebec bear hunting, I saw a most unusual vehicle called a Rokon™ (www.Rokon.com). This is basically a geared down motorcycle with a small Honda™ engine that has a chain drive to both wheels and a unique drive differential that allows the front wheel the leisure of traveling farther than the rear without placing undue stress on either. It will go places a traditional ATV can only dream about. It weighs less than two hundred pounds, will float across a creek, fits neatly on a rack on the back of my SUV, costs a third as much as a four-wheeler, and will drag two deer a mile without breaking a sweat. I still never unload my Rokon™ unless I kill something, but it's always there on the back of my truck if I need it. I load it up at the beginning of the hunting season, and it remains there until the season is over. And remember, we have a four-month-long deer season. I drag several deer from some of the most impenetrable swampy thickets you can imagine every season with my Rokon.

Given the number and variety of cargo racks available, you would think this would be a non-issue. However, I have been amazed to find that few if any are well designed. Finally, I hit upon the solution...build my own. Although I'm not much of a welder, I have a friend, Jimmy Leard, who is. Together we came up with a nifty design. The only problem was that it weighed about 150 pounds when we finished with all the features I wanted. Then, I stumbled upon a company that would build most anything you could think of from aluminum; enter CustomBilt™ Boats, or "custom-built anything" it should be. For the right price, these folks can get you what you need. To be sure, Steve Bynum, the owner and designer, has built some unique boats, but it's his aluminum racks that got my attention. They built me a custom rear rack to load and carry my Rokon as well as a fold down front rack to simultaneously carry my deer.

Aluminum rear cargo rack from Custombilt™:
http://www.boatsandfishing.com

The really nice extra features like cargo lights, an extra Class III hitch on the back of the rack, custom aluminum loading ramps, indented side panel to allow side loading, minus about a hundred pounds of extra weight make it a most unique cargo rack. I leave it on my SUV all the time. It serves very nicely as a pickup truck bed for about 95 percent of what I would ever carry in a pickup. Just give Steve Bymun at CustomBilt™ a call and tell him you want an aluminum rack like Dr. Sheppard's. He'll know what you are looking for. He built the custom rack to go on the front of my SUV for transporting deer as well.

Aluminum front rack from CustomBilt™:
http://www.boatsandfishing.com

As with most of my equipment, I tend to use it until it is worn out or fails frequently. The same is true for my vehicle. I'm still driving the same Toyota 4-Runner™ after fifteen years. It rarely breaks and is a pleasure to drive.

I keep a Warn™ winch on the front, but I'd have to admit, it is not cost effective. I can't remember the last time I needed it to get my truck out of a bind. However, should you ever need one, it immediately becomes priceless. The front rack on my SUV folds down to the ground and allows the winch cable, working through a pulley, to attach to its front side once a deer is up against it. The winch then effortlessly raises the rack (with the deer on it) to an easy-to-carry position. I can shoot a 200-pound whitetail half a mile into the woods and using my Rokon and custom racks can single handedly move him from the woods to the lodge with a minimum of effort.

The Tractor

The two pieces of equipment that have probably contributed to more of my hunting success than any other, including my gun and bow, are my dozer and tractor. Now, I realize that these may be a bit beyond most hunters' budget, but it would be hard to imagine running a hunting club without access to both. I bought my tractor, a John Deere™ 2040 with a front-end loader in 1981 new for $9,200. It is likely worth near this today. Unlike most forty-horse power tractors, the 2040 is not a utility tractor, but rather a heavy-duty farm model. It weighs in at 9,200 pounds and sports enough traction to move a heavy log from obstructing a road. Its front loader will lift more than 3,000 pounds, although I did replace the hydraulic pump with the size used on the eighty-horsepower John Deere tractor.

Rotary Cutters

A basic piece of equipment needed is a really heavy-duty rotary cutter. I destroyed two utility models before I wised up and bought a commercial grade cutter from the Bush Hog™ 406 series. This beast will devour anything a forty-horse tractor can drive over!

Disc Harrows

I would say the same about my disc harrow, the six foot Armstrong Ag™ (http://www.armstrongag.com/prodimages/9DHD). If your tractor will pull it over an object, the Armstrong™ will cut it. Just get a heavy-duty disc up front and save yourself a lot of grief, albeit an expensive savings. Sounds like something a politician would say ...an expensive savings. Just get one. You won't regret it.

Seed Drills

These handy little tools run about $1000 per foot of width. Hence, a typical eight-foot seed drill will set you back about eight grand. Nevertheless, I have become a fan of the no-tilling approach to planting food plots in the last ten years or so, and a good heavy-duty eight foot drill is by far the easiest way to plant and maintain food plots. The Sunflower™ 9010 is a good choice (http://www.sunflowermfg.com/products/). I use my disc about every fourth or fifth season. Otherwise, I run the rotary cutter over the field once in late summer, then plant using the no-till seed drill. I use a mixture of grains like wheat, rye, oats, and some red and white clovers. The seed drill has hoppers for grains that plant the seeds about two inches deep and surface drill the smaller clovers near the surface. So again, only a single pass over the field is necessary with the seed drill. We can plant about fifteen three to five-acre fields in a day's work. Wheat is cheap; so I use it. Rye is expensive but drought resistant and gives you a good stand in years when nothing else will come up. Oats are more resistant to the cold than wheat and rye and will come up and do well in the years when cold weather rolls in earlier than usual. The red clovers (like crimson) grow well during turkey season in the late winter and early spring. The white clovers (like Alyce and ladino) will do well in the summer. Given that all five of these seeds can be planted using a seed drill in a single pass, giving you forage during the entire year, the mixture is hard to beat in the South.

Dozers

My dozer is a bit of an unusual rig...a 1973 model John Deere™ 350 Wide Gauge. The JD 350 sports the same forty horsepower diesel engine as my JD 2040 tractor, and a set of extremely wide thirty inch tracks. It will go places my ATV won't go in spite of its 11,000 pounds. But venture a few inches past its limits, and you'll need to call all your neighbors to help get it unstuck! It is not large enough to push over large trees, but is invaluable for road maintenance, clean up, and making "woods roads" and shooting lanes.

JD 350 Wide Gauge Dozer

If you use a dozier much, you need to know about chains. There are chains, and then there are real chains. Go to the nearest steel retailer and tell him you want a chain cut from "grade eight" steel links. A three-eighths-inch "grade eight" chain will pull the bumper right off a vehicle. I got my JD 350 stuck once and was lucky enough to have a friend with a gigantic D-8 series Caterpillar™ nearby. We hooked my diminutive 350 to the big Cat, and he laughed at my chain when I connected to it. He said, quite condescendingly, "Son, that thing is going to snap like a sewing thread behind this D-8." From his high perch on the big Cat, he couldn't see me down inside the tiny 350's steel cage, and I was still trying to get it out of gear when he started to move. He dragged me nearly fifty yards with the tracks locked before I could get his attention enough to get him stopped. He climbed down and just stood there staring at the taut chain stretched between the two dozers. Then he said, "Son (much less demeaning now), what in hell is that thing made of? I'm sorry I didn't stop, I just kept thinking it would break and didn't notice how far we had gone!"

I suppose one final word is warranted here concerning dozers and tractors. These beasts are incredibly powerful pieces of equipment, and if you are not accustomed to being around them, I would encourage you to pay someone who is, to do the work for you, on an hourly basis. You can get yourself killed in short order running this kind of equipment. I grew up on a farm and have been running heavy equipment since I was a child. Even with this background, I almost got my due a few years back. I had rented a D-6 High Track Caterpillar™ to clear some really large stumps from a new field site. I had pushed over some big gum trees near one corner of the field and was driving them into the surrounding thicket by pushing from the root end once they were on the ground. As I started into the thicket on a certain pass, I noticed the pitch of the big Cat's engine start to tone down. Now, when the load on the blade has a D-6 in a bind enough to make it slow the engine, something is under some serious pressure! I instinctively reached for the throttle, but not in time. The six-foot high D-6 blade had a twelve-inch gum sandwiched between itself and a stump that I couldn't see off into the tree line. The tree was bowed up into a half circle and snapped just as I reached for the throttle. The butt end of it hit the steel cage about a foot to the right of my head and passed through the front of the cage, through the seat, and through the back side of the cage before it stopped against one of the cab's support posts. I shut down the engine, climbed down the tracks, and just stood there so frightened, I was nauseated. That was a defining moment for me and heavy equipment. Despite my experience, I had gained a new level of respect for their ability to get you killed.

Navigation

Perhaps more important to me than how I arrive at my hunting spot is the fact that I do arrive at my hunting spot. Long before the days of GPS, a compass was as treasured a part of my hunting gear as my bow or rifle. I came to rely upon its guidance without question. But then one night about twenty years ago, my compass finally treated me like a trusted politician. It had told me the truth just long enough that I had come to trust it completely.

For Alabama, the afternoon was cold, in the low twenties, and most of the beaver ponds and slow running creeks had at least some ice cover. I had located a small thicket created by an old logging operation that bordered a thousand acre swamp near a major river. The problem with the spot was that an approach from the south required me to cross a series of beaver pond dams and with each crossing to re-plot a path from a slightly different heading each time I crossed a body of water. It was nearly a mile from where my truck was parked. Walking in was a piece of cake in daylight, but coming out at night required one to pay careful attention to the new heading after crossing the dams in reverse order. I was perched a few feet up a sweet gum tree at the southwest corner of a small clearing near a place where a creek made a sharp bend jutting into the large swamp. Just about sundown, I heard water splashing as a heavy animal dipped into a slough off the edge of the creek. I eased my .308 Lawson to my shoulder and sat still in the biting cold. A magnificent eight-point with a crab claw antler configuration slowly visualized in the late evening vapor. He paused at the edge of an old logging road and looked back. I settled the crosshair on his shoulder and squeezed the light trigger. At dusk I was kneeling admiring the startling piece of God's creation when, for the first time, the thought of getting him out of this place came to my mind. This was in the years before I had discovered the Rokon™. My ATV was a small 90-cc version of one of Honda's early four-wheelers. The top cap of the scope on my .308 carbine had a neatly positioned compass shining up at me. I stood, gazing into the vast river bottom behind me and thought, "Well, I need to walk out, get the ATV, then drive back in, float the ATV across each of the beaver ponds at each of the dam crossings, taking care to set my headings accurately after each crossing." The first legs of the voyage went well in spite of the pitch-black night that had enveloped the vast river bottom. I was using a small, convenient ball compass now rather than the one attached to my rifle scope, and it was pinned to my shirt pocket. While navigating around the edge of a thicket on the way back, a limb snatched the compass from my shirt. For a couple of frantic moments, I was down on my knees with a flashlight searching the leaves for the crucial device. I was lucky, or so I thought. I found the compass, but the pin that held it on my shirt was gone. No problem, I thought. "I'll just lay it on the seat of my four-wheeler between my legs and glance down at it with the flashlight to keep my bearing." I made the first beaver dam crossing without a hitch. I missed the second crossing by more than a hundred yards, and that was a bit unnerving. But I knew I was past the worst obstacles, so I drove on, glancing at the compass often to make sure I was staying on course. I went far longer than I knew I should before coming to my next landmark. Suddenly I was facing a pine thicket in the velvet black of the night. I thought, "There is no pine thicket within a mile of where I was hunting!" I gazed down at my compass, looked back at the thicket, and broke out in a cold sweat. I steered the ATV slowly in a circle gazing at the compass needle and sure enough, it never moved! I picked it up, stepped off the fourwheeler and around it spun. I had been driving for nearly an hour in large circles around the vast river bottom and now had no idea where I might be. The steel frame of my four-wheeler had my compass needle lined up perfectly with its long axis, constantly pointing wherever I drove. After another hour of careful navigating, I finally came out on a road that got me back to my truck. You should have seen the look on the guys' faces when I arrived back at the lodge with a deer sporting no hair. I had dragged him several miles through the river swamp and dragged off most of the hair from both his sides. He looked like a scalded pig by the time I reached the truck. Johnny Lanier, one of Bent Creek Lodge's owners, in his usual dry wit gazed thoughtfully for a moment at the hairless animal and finally asked, "Bob, did you get far enough off the road this afternoon?"

About a month later, I was hunting the same area late one evening and took a magnificent nine point on a slough near this same swamp. However, this time, my trusty four-wheeler had a carburetor problem, and I would be faced with dragging this 220-pound beast more than a mile by hand. With the last fiasco fresh on my mind, I stood for several minutes admiring the animal, but perplexed as to just how I would get him out of here. Finally, I picked up my .308 Lawson, turned, and gazed for a moment across the river bottom in the direction of my truck. I looked down at my compass. I had two beaver ponds and a creek to cross, not to mention the vast distance. The weather was typical January in Alabama, about twenty-five degrees. I decided he would be just fine in the woods until the following morning. With the light of day, I could reach him shortly after daylight and have the entire morning to drag him out. I decided to say nothing when I got back to the lodge. However, as we sat devouring a typical sumptuous Bent Creek meal, one of the hunters at the table to my right asked, "Doc, did you see anything this afternoon?" I didn't want to flat-out lie, so I said without looking up, "Well, I did shoot, but he's in a really bad place. I'll need to go back in for him tomorrow. My ATV is broken, and I'll need to drag him by hand." But the gentleman just wouldn't let it go. He countered, "Hey, we'll go back with you tonight and get him!" I resisted, "Oh no, he'll be fine until morning." He would not have it. "Not a chance. We'll go as soon as we finish eating. I have a brand-new ATV we can take." I tried again, "But he's across several beaver ponds and the ATV will have to be floated across the water. That's the way I do it with my four-wheeler." He countered, "My ATV will float. I'm certain it will." I could see I was losing the argument and finally conceded, "Okay, if you insist, we'll try it." By this point, half a dozen or more hunters were eagerly preparing for the adventure. We piled into two pickups and were off to the river bottom. We unloaded the ATV (a new Honda Big Red™), and the loud crowd marched off into the velvet black swamp, flashlights flashing in all directions and making enough racket to run every deer from this area for the next two seasons. I thought to myself, "Man, I should have kept my mouth shut. I'll never see another deer in this area again."

Tell Me It'll Float!

About half a mile from the truck, we came to the crossing on the creek. There was a pretty broad-based beaver dam that had been there for several seasons. Upstream from the dam was a pool of water about thirty feet across and about eight feet deep. The banks on either side left the water in a gentle slope. I explained to the gracious gentleman that I usually just tied a rope to the front of my ATV, eased it off into the pool, then walked the beaver dam holding onto the rope. Once on the far side, I slowly pulled it up onto the bank. From there, I was home free. On the return trip, I would drag the deer across the dam and reverse the process. He said excitedly, "Okay, sounds like a plan to me!" We left the ATV running with its headlight on, attached the rope, and eased it off into the pool. I gave the rope plenty of slack. To all our chagrin, it immediately flipped upside down and sank like a rock! I just stood there speechless holding the rope in front of me. All we could see was the ATV's headlight shining up from the murky creek bottom. I turned to face his flashlight and suggested sort of lightheartedly, "Okay. Perhaps it won't float." He was not laughing.

We fished the muddy ATV from the creek, turned it over, and half

the crowd worked on getting the water out of the fuel lines while the other half of us trekked across the beaver ponds and retrieved the buck by hand. By the time we returned to the creek, it was nearing midnight, but they had the ATV running, albeit not smoothly. A couple of years later, the gracious gent told me the ATV never really recovered and that he had sold it. He was still not laughing, and I felt really awful about the mishap. I've never again made the mistake of seeking help getting my deer out of the ridiculous places I tend to hunt. The Rokon™ has pretty much resolved any difficulty of retrieving a deer from the depths of these vast Southern swamps I frequent.

I will admit that I have always been intrigued with gadgets, particularly those that make life easier, or allow us to do things we couldn't do without them. When Motorola™ was doing their initial market surveys before bringing one of the first handheld GPS devices to the market, I was working with several manufacturers, testing equipment during pre-market analysis and was asked to use one of these gadgets and report what I thought the basic functionality should include. Although amazed at what this thing could do, I was enough of a hunter to know that it should do only one thing well, "Point me back to the truck." In other words, unlike my compass, which insists on pointing toward the north pole where I have no desire to go, here was a device with the ability to point one toward his vehicle, regardless of how tortuous a course he wished to take in getting there. I was dumbfounded to find that neither Motorola nor any of the other manufacturers programmed this basic common sense functionality into their devices for several generations of units. Only in the last couple of years will they now perform this basic function and even now, they don't display it well on their overly complex interface. Nevertheless, the modern handheld GPS is an invaluable device to the hunter. However, I'll admit that I still don't use one for basic navigation to and from my hunting spots. The size is too large and the interface is still far too complex and cluttered. A pin on compass is just too simple and effective to beat...at least when kept away from steel objects! I use my GPS (a Garmin™ Nuvi 500 series—a slightly larger but waterproof device that doubles as an off-road and on-road navigation tool) to mark the longitude/latitude coordinates of my spots for entry into a database of my hunting stand sites. (To download a free copy of my hunting database software, go to my Web site, www.BobSheppard.com and follow the hunting links.)

Computers

In spite of my fascination with gadgets, I was a bit of a latecomer to the age of the computer. I ignored the early PC versions including all of Apple's popular offerings such as the IIe. But by the mid-1980s I began to realize this was no fad. I bought one of the first versions of the Mac, a dazzling beast sporting two floppy drives (one to run the OS and one to hold your data files) and an eight-inch black and white screen. These were the days before "hard drives" had been invented and of course, before the Internet existed. Each floppy held a whopping 1.4 megabytes of data. But the trend was set. Storage capacity and processor speed were destined to double about every eighteen months for many years to come. And along with these strengths would come the ability to change our lives forever. By the late 1980s, the Internet was born and life on earth left orbit never to return. I taught myself to do basic programming, and one of the first programs I developed was a database designed to house the location of all my hunting spots contained on hundreds of three-by-five-inch index cards filling several shoe boxes underneath my bed. With the advent of the GPS, I added latitude/longitude coordinates to the database and these became the framework of where and how I would hunt for two decades.

The way I utilize this database of information is really quite simple. I check the weather and wind direction for the following day, then go to the database and do a search for all my stand sites, within the particular area I'm planning to hunt that can be hunted effectively utilizing the wind direction predicted for that day. For example, let's say I was planning to hunt the Whitfield section of land at Bent Creek Lodge (www.BentCreekLodge.com) tomorrow morning during bow season, and that the wind for tomorrow is predicted to be northwest. I would create a search query that locates: Bent Creek Lodge/Whitfield/Bow/AM/Northwest. The database would then present me with a found set of potential hunting spots meeting these descriptors from which I could choose a single spot. You would be surprised how often good spots can fade from your memory when you haven't hunted them recently. This approach has the added benefit of helping you avoid over hunting your good spots. If you utilize a GPS for navigation, my hunting database (www.BobSheppard.com and follow the download links) will not only contain a photo or graphic representation of the spot with its coordinates but a file containing the series of waypoints and routes to get there. Just download it from your PC to your GPS and you are ready to go.

Shooting Houses

In the South, what we call "shooting houses" have become a standard approach for field hunting. My adaptation of the "shooting lanes" has also allowed the use of these small, watertight containers to be effectively used throughout the day. They are small, ranging in size from about thirty-by-thirty inches to as large as six-by-eight feet. There are a multitude of versions made from a range of materials on the market now. Nevertheless, I tend to build my own because I like to set up a shooting bench fitted to my rifle and shooting height in each one. If you visit my Website (www.BobSheppard.com), you can follow the hunting links to a set of plans one can use for their simple construction utilizing materials found at any local building materials store.

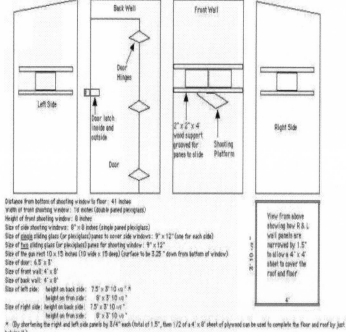

Distance from bottom of shooting window to floor: 41 inches
Width of front shooting window: 14 inches (double paned plexiglass)
Height of front shooting window: 6 inches
Size of side shooting windows: 6" x 8 inches (single paned plexiglass)
Size of single sliding glass (or plexiglass) panes to cover side windows: 9" x 12" (one for each side)
Size of two sliding glass (or plexiglass) panes for shooting window: 9" x 12"
Size of the gun rest 10 x 15 inches (10 wide x 15 deep) (surface to be 3.25 " down from bottom of window)
Size of door: 6.5' x 3'
Size of front wall: 4' x 8'
Size of back wall: 4' x 8'
Size of left side: height on back side: 7.5' x 3' 10 in " *
                     height on front side: 8' x 3' 10 in "
Size of right side; height on back side: 7.5' x 3' 10 in ".
                     height on front side: 8' x 3' 10 in ".
* (By shortening the right and left side panels by 3/4" each (total of 1.5", then 1/2 of a 4' x 8' sheet of plywood can be used to complete the floor and roof by just halving it.)
Size of top: 4' x 4'
Size of floor: 4' x 4'
Shooting platform size: 2" x 8" x 10" (It's top surface should be 3" below the bottom of the window. It can be secured into place by metal shelving brackets.

* We generally use galvanized thin 1" x 1" angle to fasten the walls to each other and to fasten the walls to the floor and to the roof using 1" dry wall screws
* The house should then be set up on four concrete blocks to keep the floor from rotting.
* The thickness of the plywood and whether it is weather treated are optional, but I recommend using 5/8" thickness at a minimum and preferably 3/4" and using treated wood for longevity.
* Two sheets of tin will generally cover the top, although this is optional.

238

All you need is a saw and screwdriver to build one. The cost runs about $300 for the four-by-four-foot version. They are quiet, dry, warm, and most comfortable. I recommend rimming the door with aluminum channel in order to avoid warp and poor sealing when closed. This is not really necessary for warmth but will go a long way toward keeping vermin and wasps out of the house during the summer months. The wasps particularly come to life when you light a heater in December and really take offense to your interrupting their hibernation.

Shooting house sitting on a shooting lane

All the above notwithstanding, let's be clear and honest here. Should someone ask you how much your venison costs per pound, first you should quickly point out that, like precious metals, this delicacy is not even considered in such gross measurements as pounds. Ounces perhaps ...more apt, grams. My best guess is somewhere in the range of four dollars per gram. Maybe. On a good, cold, clear, windy day!

The Experienced Hunter

I want to be fair here to the young hunter. To do so, I must explain that there is a part of what I would attempt to teach about hunting that simply must be learned in the field. I hope I have helped you conceptualize what a good ambush spot might look like, how to locate one and when and under what conditions you might hunt that spot. But the truth is, if I took you to the woods in the right weather conditions, but with no personal experience and placed you in exactly the right tree, faced you the right direction, and told you where the deer would appear, you would not likely kill the first dozen deer to come by you. Knowing when to take the shot, when you can move, and when you must remain perfectly still is crucial. One must know how to read the animal and this comes only with making mistakes in the woods and learning from them. This part of hunting is hard to teach. I made some attempt with my children by taking them with me. They would climb the same tree I was in. I would point out the deer when he appeared, talk constantly, albeit softly, to them as the deer approached. I would say, "When he gets to the downfall just past the holly bush, I'll draw and take him." If the deer should change directions, I would quickly verbally rebuild the scenario. By watching and

242

listening to me in this way, they learned skills needed to execute that last minute before the shot that would take most hunters a decade to master. After some shots, I climb down immediately to go after the deer. With others, I know to wait an hour or more, quietly climb down and come back the following morning to track the deer. Only experience can teach the skill of knowing which action to take. We even have some numbers that would suggest what statistical likelihood of success these final moment skills impart on the hunter's success. All the other factors being equal, an experienced hunter's odds of bringing an animal back to camp is about 30 percent higher than that of an unskilled hunter. I can't begin to tell you of the hundreds of deer I have run off trying to execute that last thirty seconds, particularly using a bow and arrow. The older the deer, the more likely he is to pick up on any little mistake you make. A sudden movement at the wrong instant. An unnatural noise when the animal is close. An arrow dropping off the arrow rest as you draw. Even a subtle move when the deer is close and looking up at you. These things can just destroy your success and your confidence. They must be mastered to become consistently successful.

Allow me to illustrate with an example. Many years ago, I was hunting on the edge of the Tombigbee River near the Vienna boat landing. I was about two miles up the river in a narrow strip of timber that lay between one of the dredge/spoil areas and the river edge. About sundown a buck came strolling into view. He was an animal on a mission. I don't know where he was headed, but he seemed to have no hesitation about getting there. He never stopped walking from moment I first got a glimpse of him until he was ten yards in front of me. He was going to pass directly underneath me, and I knew what would happen if he got to the base of the tree and smelled where I had kneeled to prepare for the climb. When he paused directly in front of me, there was no hint of cover. He was staring at ground level past my location, but I knew better than to move. He would have looked up, and in an instant, it would have been over. He was simply too close. I sat in a frozen position, waiting for an opportunity, but none was apparent. Off to the north of us several hundred yards, a crappie fisherman was entering the river from a slough. His outboard hit a stump or submerged log and the foot of the motor popped up out of the water and made a sudden loud chattering sound. The buck jerked his head around focusing his attention in that direction. Because I had the experience of having executed these last few seconds so many times, I knew what to do instantly. When his head swung, I made a quick, but smooth draw. In a few rapid heartbeats, he was mine. I was in the right place, under the right conditions, facing the right direction, and expecting the animal to appear from where he did. I was standing having addressed his approach before he was close and had my bow up and ready to draw. Yet, under the circumstances, I knew to remain still even though he was getting far too close. He just never gave me a shot until he was on top of me. Had he started to walk again, I would have drawn while he walked as he would start to pass under me, but knowing that he would freeze, then bolt when he smelled my presence. I would settle the pin to break his spine and release at the instant he froze. So, even though he gave me an easy lethal shot, I had a backup plan if he forced the issue. Knowing the details of the myriad ways of executing those last few seconds must be learned by trial and error for most of us. And it takes years to accomplish. I would just encourage the young hunter not to let the mistakes get under your skin.

Years ago, a hunting buddy was listening to me talk to some of

his club members about the odds of recovering a deer after making the shot. One of the hunters had made a reasonable shot but couldn't find the deer. He and his friends had made a really concerted effort to scour the area for any sign of the deer, but to no avail. I made the following statement, "Well, it's been my

245

experience that I get a good shot at about half the deer I see. Of the ones I shoot at, I recover about half, maybe a little better."There are just too many things that can go wrong in that last few seconds before and during the shot. The animal can react to something he saw or heard that you have little if any control over. Even with a perfect hit, the animal may cross water, enter a virtually impenetrable thicket or double back, and you not catch it in your tracking. Granted, this was during my years of hunting with a recurve. When a deer is hit by a full-length arrow, the broadhead passes easily through and the shot is a lethal one, but the deer is spooked and when he starts to run, the arrow is slapping every bush he passes. The result is that he runs full tilt until he dies. In twenty to thirty seconds, he can cover 300 yards or more before expiring.This is contrasted with a typical shot from a short arrowed compound. The arrow passes through, and sticks in the ground past the deer. He bounces a few yards, stops, and looks back. Within the same twenty to thirty seconds, he wobbles and falls over, often in sight of the hunter.

My friend listened and said nothing for a long while. Finally, now visibly frustrated, he said, "Dr. Bob, I hate to be argumentative, but I just don't understand why you lose so many deer. I know you are a skilled tracker, and I've seen you shoot. But I have taken seven deer with my bow, and I have never failed to recover one."

A bit to his surprise, I said, "I agree. I've done that many times. But let's talk again when you have taken fifty deer. You will be singing a different tune indeed."

That was the end of the discussion, but he was not convinced. About the middle of the gun season the following year, we crossed paths at one of the gates coming out from the woods one evening. Alone, he approached my truck and looked dejected.

He softly offered, "I need to tell you something. Do you remember last year when you were telling me about the odds of recovering the deer I hit with a bow?"

"I do," I countered. "Why do you ask?"

"Well, it's almost like voodoo, but I've lost the last five deer I put an arrow through! It's like I can't do anything right."

"Relax," I said. "I know the purists and the animal rights activists don't want to hear it, but these are simply the facts. I'd love to tell you that if you do everything right, you would find all these deer. But I'd simply be lying to you. Reality simply dictates otherwise. I got through stretches of fifteen to twenty deer without losing one at times, but sooner or later, the odds catch up with you. Shots taken with the deer close and particularly slightly quartering away, will often look like a perfect shot, but in reality will pass between the shoulder and the chest cavity and will not prove to be lethal. Shots straight down, if they fail to break the spinal cord will knock the deer onto the ground, but he will jump up and that will be the last you will see of him. Animals angling toward you have a large part of their vitals covered by the scapula, and if the ridge of that bone is hit, even the heaviest compound will not penetrate deep enough for a lethal shot. You have a perfect sight picture, but during that brief period of concentration before you release, the animal starts to move and takes a step forward, allowing for penetration too far back. This will be a long and often fruitless tracking job. These things just happen."

My friend left the discussion a sobered and more seasoned hunter.

I make no excuse for the realities of bow hunting. Taking only high percentage shots do not solve the problems. I fully intend to kill every animal I take a shot at. But we must be honest with the facts. If you take a lot of deer with a bow, just brace yourself for this reality. It will happen. You will not avoid it. If you stumble across a purist who insists otherwise, just relax. If he hunts enough, the odds will teach him better.

Ballistics

This may get a little technical for you, but it is an important aspect of hunter experience. Most hunters really don't understand what happens when a bullet leaves their barrel or what an arrow does when it leaves a bow. Both have a lot in common. Relative to the line of sight, the bullet/arrow will likely rise simply because we have the gun or bow aimed upward relative to the line of sight. However, neither projectile ever rises relative to the earth's gravitational pull. Let me put this another way. If you could with enough precision, drop a lead bullet from one hand and pull the trigger of a gun aimed toward the horizon at exactly the same instant with the other hand, both bullets will hit the ground at exactly the same instant! It would not even matter if the bullets were a different weight! These bullets are simply obeying Newton's laws of gravity.

When you shoot a rifle, the bullet rises rapidly relative to the line of sight you see when looking through the scope, and within about twenty to forty yards, crosses the line of sight on its way up. It will arc upward, and at some point, typically at about eighty to eighty-five yards for most centerfire cartridges, will reach the high point of its trajectory. If the gun is sighted in at 100 yards, it will drop back through the line of sight at 100 yards (the sight in distance). At a surprisingly short distance past that, it will drop several inches below the line of sight...typically at about 140 to 150 yards. Sighted in at 100 yards, you may hold the crosshair on the center of a whitetail's kill zone, which is about ten inches in diameter, and hit within that ten-inch kill zone regardless of whether the animal is ten yards or 110 yards from you. However, when you start to reach on out there to distances beyond 200 yards with most centerfire cartridges, you must make some alterations, or perhaps aim high on the target. The latter is always risky shooting. When I was asking the near impossible of my hot loaded 30–06 Colt-Sauer™, I had to optimize this variation of rise and fall of the bullet relative to the line of sight. To do this, I sighted the gun in at 300 yards. Set at such an extreme distance, the bullet would cross the line of sight on its way up at twenty-three yards. It would reach the high point in its arc of 4.7 inches at 187 yards. It would fall back through the line of sight at 300 yards (the sight in distance). It would fall 4.7 inches below the line of sight at 353 yards. Hence with this hot-loaded 30-caliber cartridge generating about 3000 fps muzzle velocity, I could hold dead on the target from zero to 353 yards and know that I would be within 4.7 inches of that point of aim regardless of where along that bullet path the deer was standing. But go just a few yards past that 350-yard mark, and the bullet would pass completely underneath the deer's body. Should you hold the least bit too high on a deer, you could easily shoot over him at 185 yards. My move to the 300 Remington Ultramag™ flattened out this bullet trajectory a modest amount, but at the expense of some serious recoil and more than twice the powder charge. Moving up on bullet size to achieve a better ballistic coefficient at 165 grains and driving the boat tail spitzer at a sizzling 3500 fps the following ballistics can be achieved. The bullet crosses the line of sight on its way up at thirty-five yards. It reaches the peak of its arc upward at 196 yards at 4.4 inches and falls back through the line of sight at 340 yards (now the sight in distance). It falls 4.4 inches below the line of sight at 400 yards. By more than doubling the powder charge (and the recoil), we get a very modest improvement in trajectory. The bullet velocity at 400 yards for this hot magnum is comparable to a .308 Winchester™ at the muzzle. However, I can assure you that all this academic talk about ballistics is not worth a cent unless you can hit what you are shooting at given these extended distances. And most hunters cannot. I have taken scores of hunters to my shooting range, and had them shoot their guns at half this distance (200 yards). Eight out of ten of them cannot hit a ten-inch circle at this distance with three shot groups! So, first, don't fool yourself. If you can't shoot well enough to hit a deer sized target at 200 yards, why punish yourself with a magnum caliber to achieve this extra edge in ballistics? I've discussed in some detail elsewhere in this book how to tame a heavy magnum cartridge like the 300 RUM. And by the way, a 300 RUM is not a belted magnum cartridge, but by anyone's standards is still a "magnum" cartridge. If you would like to play around with these ballistic concepts, go to Norma's Web site and plug in the ballistics of your favorite cartridge (http://www.norma.cc/sortimentladd.asp?doc=Sort&Lang=2#). Go to the drop-down menu under the menu bar item "Ballistic" and choose "Ballistic US."This is an incredibly helpful visual demonstration of typical centerfire ballistics when you are trying to work up loads for a particular purpose.

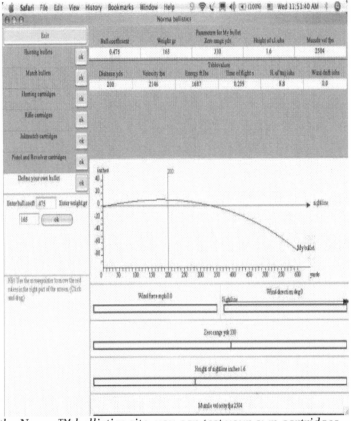

At the Norma™ ballistics site, you can test your own cartridges.

I think a far more productive exercise for most hunters is simply to learn to shoot better at any distance. How can we do this? Well, it's not as difficult as you might imagine. The most important things to focus upon are:

1) A good trigger—no creep, no overtravel, and relatively light weight (three pounds or less).

2) An accurate rifle—Your gun should be capable of at least 1.5 MOA (minutes of angle). This means it should shoot at least a 1.5-inch group or less at 100 yards. For practical purposes, if it shoots 1.5 inches at 100 yards, it will shoot a six-inch group at 300 yards! If it will shoot a one-inch group at 100 yards, it will shoot a four-inch group at 300 yards. To hit a ten-inch target consistently at 400 yards, you need a half MOA of accuracy. That means half-inch groups at 100 yards.

3) A solid brace—You need both the forepiece and the buttstock of your gun solidly braced. It is simply not good enough to place the forepiece of the rifle in the shooting house window and the buttstock against your shoulder. Not one in a hundred hunters can hit a ten inch circle at 400 yards with this kind of rest. For that matter, not even at 300 yards. In your own shooting houses, take the time to put a shelf across the front of the shooting house just underneath the window to allow sandbags to be placed under and on both sides of the buttstock. If you are visiting where you just don't have a

buttstock brace, make one to keep with you by taking a piece of ski rope and weaving it back through itself to make a slip knot on each end. Place a sharp pointed small eye bolt screw on either end of the rope (about five feet long). Screw each eye bolt into the sides of the shooting house or into the wall over the window and allow your rifle's buttstock to rest on the rope, pulling the rope into a V-shape such that the bottom of the "V" is behind the pistol grip part of the buttstock. The weight of the gun holds it in position. When you add the weight of your arm and face resting on the buttstock, it forms a rock solid brace rivaling a bench with sand bags. Take up the slack using the slipknot to allow for an aim on the horizon. It adjusts to any angle of shooting virtually instantly. I have taken many deer out to a quarter mile with this rig. It weighs less than three ounces and will fit in your shirt pocket.

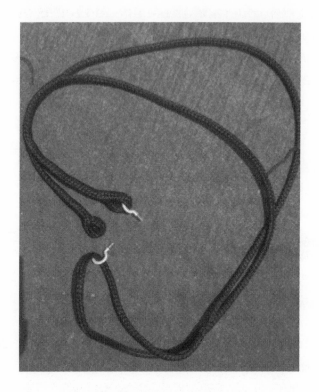

Rope-based shooting brace leaves no excuse for missing at extended distances.

Practice

I have spent some time elsewhere defining the details of how to practice shooting with a bow, but allow me to adapt this style of practice to a rifle. My first approach is to work up a load that optimizes accuracy with bullet velocity, and therefore trajectory, of my cartridge/rifle combination. Once this is done, I rarely, if ever, change it again. By the time I finish working up a load, I have also sighted in my gun for its optimal sight in distance. As I mentioned, for the 300 Remington Ultramag™, that is about 340 yards. For my short barreled .308 Winchester™, the sight in distance is 200 yards. This gives me a two-inch high point in the trajectory and a fall of four inches below the line of sight at 250 yards. By extending the sight in distance, I could squeeze out another fifty yards out of the setup with a four-inch high point in the trajectory, but why do this? At 250 yards, the bullet velocity is down around 2200 fps and the energy is well below 2000 foot/pounds. This will lead to long-tracking jobs and a lot of lost animals. I use my .308 for "woods hunting" where shots are typically less than 100 yards and killing capacity is still at an acceptable level.

So how do I practice? Well, to be honest, I don't. Unlike with my bow where a little shooting (one shot per day) is helpful, I can shoot my rifle just fine without firing it for months. But just to give me the confidence that my scope is on, and that nothing is wrong with my gun nor cartridges, I shoot one round at a 100 to 200 yard target about once per week throughout the entire season. If that round hits within half an inch of the bull's-eye, I know it will do its job if I do mine. I've found that every few years, my scope will have worked loose, or a batch of repetitively reloaded cartridges will start to develop case failures, or something will happen that requires a correction. Mostly though, the shot a week plan just gives me the confidence that I can take just about any animal I can see. This all figures quite nicely into the well-rounded knowledge base of an experienced hunter.

Confessions of a Sinful Hunter

This was a tough chapter for me to bring to paper. Confessing the truth is often sobering, particularly when it is sometimes an unpleasant truth. But I think it is necessary because otherwise, one might have left this book thinking that I did everything perfectly in learning to become a successful whitetail hunter. Such is just not the case. I made a lot of mistakes, many over and over again.

When Passion Is Too Much

Both of our children, Dusty and Molly, love to hunt. Both also love to fish. In fact, they simply love the outdoors. Dustin, our first child, caught the brunt of my initial frustrated efforts to sort out the whitetail's world. I hunted hard and often pushed him too hard. In doing so, I pushed him away from the sport to a degree. He enjoys deer hunting but does not share my burning passion. If the weather doesn't cooperate, he'd just as soon catch a few bass. That is likely because he and I spent thousands of hours sharing a small jon boat. Today, he is a seasoned, formally trained emergency medicine physician and has learned to tackle one disaster after another in a very hostile environment with little ruffling of his feathers. Molly has never allowed herself to take life too seriously and, as such, has no trouble enjoying whatever joy comes her way. Both are wonderful kids and have seasoned my life with far more joy than anguish, their teenage years notwithstanding!

One morning when Dust, as I fondly call him, and I were turkey hunting together, we had located a gobbler that was ripping and snorting up and down a patch of road near a clear cut. I placed Dust right at the edge of the clear cut at a place where the road made a sharp turn. I knew that if I stayed well behind him and up the hill a piece, the gobbler would walk down the road right into his lap. Everything went perfectly until the gobbler got to the turn in the road. As these vermin will do sometimes for no clear reason, he stopped and decided to make a stand here. He paced in a short place on the road for nearly an hour. I could see him from where I was, but he was just out of Dusty's line of sight. I retreated up the hill another hundred yards, called louder, called with a gobble box, called with a variety of mouth calls, slates, and boxes, but all to no avail. He just wasn't going to budge. Finally Dust just couldn't take it anymore, and I saw him when he got up. He walked up the hill toward me, and I had the answer ready. As soon as he got to me, I said, "Don't sweat it, Dust. I hear another bird gobbling across the valley up on that next hill." I cupped my years in that direction and insisted, "Hear him?"

To this gesture, only a teenager could top, he instantly cupped

his ear back in the direction of the truck and said, "Dad, do you hear that?" I listened, fully expecting that his superior hearing had located yet an easier bird gobbling. Nothing. I didn't hear a thing. He insisted, cupping his ears again, now leaning convincingly in that direction, "Hear that biscuit calling me to breakfast?"

When Dust was about five, he kept pestering me to take him deer hunting with me. Those were the years I spent glassing large soybean fields. Finally, I gave in. It was a cold, misty, soggy day, so I decided to take a sleeping bag figuring he would lose interest pretty quickly, and then I could just pack him away in a warm dry place in the weeds behind me. Things went pretty well as planned, but I found myself venturing out into an untilled field up to an old fence line in order to get a closer look at an eight-point that had entered the bean field nearly a quarter mile away. I crawled through the wet weeds with Dust and the sleeping bag in tow. It took me nearly an hour to close the gap on the big whitetail. As I got closer, I could tell he was a really nice animal, and my focus intensified. Finally, I parked Dust in patch of switch weed near the fence line and tucked him away in the sleeping bag. By now, it was drizzling rain. I had gotten about as close as I could get to the deer without him seeing my movement through the fence line. So I kneeled near a post and planned to wait him out. Indeed he fed closer and closer. Just about the time the deer was venturing within my 300-yard limit, I heard what sounded like a choking cat in the weeds behind me. I slowly lowered my head and crawled back to the bag. Dust was soaked, freezing, and now crying in the soggy sleeping bag. "Dad, I wanna go home!" he sputtered. I peered back through the fence line, gave up on making the shot, and started the trek back to the truck. That day probably took more out of his zeal for hunting than all the good times combined. I simply pushed him too hard when he was too young to understand what was driving me.

Our daughter, Molly, born when Dusty was nearly ten, got the

benefit of many of the mistakes I made in the earlier years. I took Molly deer hunting for the first time when she was also about five. But she saw the game from a very different perspective. She was sitting with me in a ladder stand one morning at the end of a slough when two deer came slipping cautiously by us off to her side of the tree. I leaned into the .308 thumbhole

Lawson™ and said, "Hold your ears, Mollycule," as I called her. I squeezed the trigger. One of the deer hit the dirt where it stood, and the other bounded a few yards and stopped to look back.

She looked up at me through big blue eyes and said indignantly, "Well, shoot the other one, Daddy!" She loves to hunt to this day.

When Molly was eleven, I took her to Bent Creek Lodge for a deer hunt for her birthday. We sat watching the edge of an old field that bordered a swampy river bottom as the biting northwest wind howled around us. About sundown two respectable eight points appeared from the northwest corner of the clearing. At eleven, she was ready to take something and I was about to let her when I caught some movement back to the northeast. A magnificent ten point topped the rise and slowly started to make his way toward us. Honestly, I don't know who was the most nervous. As the big bruiser passed closest to us, we had both rifles on him. Molly was shooting my .308 Cochise™ thumbhole custom Lawson, and I had a Colt-Sauer ™ 30–06 centering his chest. I said as quietly and smoothly as I could, "Okay, whenever you are rea—." Blam! I never got "ready" from my mouth. To both our surprise, the heavy animal hit the dirt like a sack of potatoes. She gleamed over the scope and screamed in a high-pitched, obviously surprised voice, "I got him!" By the time we got him loaded onto the rack on the front of my truck, it was dark and drizzling rain.

Molly celebrating her twenty-first birthday.

We drove a few miles around to where Dusty was hunting and found that he had taken a nice eight-point as well. As he cleared the headlights of his truck so he could see the front rack of my truck, he exclaimed, "Jiminy Crickets, Dad. That is a monster." Just about the time he finished the statement, he paused, stared at the huge animal for a brief moment, and exclaimed in disbelief, "No, Dad. Tell me she didn't kill this!" He scored in the 140's, a most respectable animal for

Alabama. Of course, she never misses an opportunity to goad her big brother about it.

Hunting Too Hard

When one is driven by a passion for success, it is often easy to over do the passion. I've seen classmates through college and medical school so intensely focused on their studies, that they simply lost the skill of enjoying life. They worked to the exclusion of even those closest to them. I did well in school academically, but never lost sight of the healthy balance between work and play. The dean of the school of medicine where I trained would often snarl to my fellow residents, "He could be a world-class physician were it not for those damn bass!" He did his best to make an academician out of me, but the call of the wild was just too strong in those early years. Oddly enough, I am now an associate professor of internal medicine teaching at the University of Alabama School of Medicine and have won best teaching awards for the last seven years running. Chief, maybe there's hope for me yet!

However, when it came to fishing and hunting, I too have been guilty of just pushing the envelope too hard. I hunted and fished to the exclusion of my family's happiness, particularly in the early years of my marriage. I finally eased my foot of the pedal after I got a little older and have enjoyed some wonderful years with both my kids and with my wife, Brenda, who's been at my side for more than thirty-five years. She is my dearest friend, my closest buddy, the love of my life, and the person with whom I am content to finish my years on this earth.

I remember about twenty years ago finally talking her into going turkey hunting with me one morning. We were lucky enough to get on a bird early in the morning, and I was so excited, I could hardly contain myself. I called, and he echoed back. After nearly an hour of teasing and coaxing, I could tell he was ever so slowly inching closer with each pass. The hill sloped down steeply in front of us, so he had to get to within about twenty yards before I could see his head peek above the horizon. Finally, it happened. I saw movement from behind a bush. I tightened the trigger and when he cleared the bush, I flattened him. To my surprise, Brenda bounced to her feet, and exclaimed in a high-pitched, desperate voice, "Get him, and let's go. I'm freezing!" I just sat there dumbfounded. How could anyone be cold amidst such excitement? She did actually come to relish bass fishing after we built our own lake ...basically when the fishing got easier and more convenient. But, still, if they don't act right in short order, she'll break out a book and ignore them without hesitation.

In addition to being hard on one's family, hunting too hard can

cause you to commit other sins. For example, you have heard me say repeatedly in this book how important it is not to over hunt a good spot. Hunting your spots with the wind marginal or simply wrong can deteriorate your success on the good days. Being in the woods so much leaves your scent scattered through the whitetail's habitat, and he takes it seriously by simply becoming more and more nocturnal. He makes tracks and rubs and scrapes as usual ...all at night.

One of the regretful mistakes from the early years of my hunting was the placement of dozens of ladder stands scattered through the best spots on my hunting club. Little did I realize that I was simply advertising to my hunting companions where I was hunting. Worse than that, they were hunting from my stands when I wasn't there! This added hunting pressure made the herd more nocturnal in general, but worse, it made the deer in the area avoid the very places from which I was trying to ambush them.

One morning some twenty years ago, I had a place tucked into the backside of a thicket on the Tombigbee River that I had been saving back for just the right conditions. I had labored for days during the hot summer cutting three-foot wide shooting lanes into the thicket. A few days before Christmas, the wind was perfect. The spot required that I launch my boat in the river, motor upstream a few miles and approach the stand from the downwind side from the river. When I got to the stand, I sat all morning and saw nothing. Surprised, I started to climb down about noon and give it up. I noticed something white protruding from the edge of the canvas seat. I pulled it out to find a hunting buddy's business card with a note on the back, "Great spot. Hope you don't mind me hunting it." I made the run back down river, loaded my boat, and spent the next two weeks removing all my ladder stands from the woods. I had worked hundreds of hours cutting the shooting lanes where those ladder stands were set up. It was a hard lesson, but one I learned well. I have never left a tree stand in the woods where I hunt since.

Another aspect of this hunting too hard that I touched on is

hunting when the conditions are not right. For many years I hunted desperately hard, but just couldn't understand why I took very few older age class bucks. There were several factors coming to bear on my mixed success. The state of Alabama had no deer left following the Great Depression of the 1930s except for a tiny isolated herd on a private tract of land near Demopolis, Alabama. It was commonly referred to as Shady Grove Plantation, having been a farming plantation in the 1800s. From this small herd, the state of Alabama was restocked during the 1950s.

By the late 1970s and early 1980s, we had nearly a million whitetails and a liberal deer-per-day bag limit. Shortly thereafter, it would increase to two deer per day. No one knew much about quality herd management, and we had just come from an era when there were no animals to hunt. It was considered shameful to shoot a doe, even when the biologists were doing their best to convince us to take some of them out of the rapidly expanding herds. Dog hunting was the rage then and virtually no one would shoot a doe. As a result, we had a dense whitetail population with a buck-to-doe ratio in the one-to-twelve range. What bucks were present were cropped off as soon as they hatched out. Amongst us hunters, it was a numbers game. We took as many bucks as we could each season. It was not unusual in those days for a good rifle hunter to take fifteen bucks in a season. Little did most of my club members know, I often took that many deer with my bow before the gun season came in! Once the gun season was in, anything with ivory above the hairline was reduced to possession. So this combination of our taking the bucks at a very young age, combined with the intense hunting pressure made taking an older age class animal a difficult task indeed. Looking back, I'd like to think I would do it differently. But the truth is, anyone allowing a yearling buck to walk in those days would likely see him on someone's tailgate within a few days. We took 60 to 70 percent of the entire herd of bucks every season. There was just no opportunity for a buck to reach maturity. By the late 1980s and early 1990s, there were pockets of "quality management" beginning to emerge and as I learned more and more about hunting, I began to seek these quality habitats out.

I mentioned earlier that I had probably spent more time learning to become a successful whitetail hunter than I had studying to become a physician. The statistical odds of a single individual becoming a physician in America is somewhere in the 0.2 percent range. I have never seen any published numbers on the number of whitetail hunters who have taken more than a thousand animals, but I suspect you have enough fingers to count them. The odds of achieving this kind of success would be something like 0.000004 percent! Again, looking back, I wish I had been more selective, but the facts remain what they are. I am a shooter and, therefore, waiting for something that virtually did not exist in our area was deemed fruitless, and rightly so. During the 2008–09 season, I took only one whitetail with a gun, but turned down more than a hundred animals most hunters would have taken and mounted. In the last ten years, I have become extremely selective during the rifle and black powder seasons, but when I'm bowhunting, the first animal to come by me gets a free ride to the lodge. I just absolutely love the challenge of taking these animals with a bow.

So, why did I write this book? Well, America is changing. I am sadly fearful that my children will see sport hunting fade from our culture in the next few decades, much as it has in Europe. I am told we still have more than eleven million whitetail hunters in America, but hunting license sales are declining annually. With much of our culture centered in the urban landscape, individuals with the amount of experience I have amassed are rare even today. A person who is blessed enough to have lived in a part of the country with a huge whitetail herd, an incredibly liberal bag limit, and having had the income and leisure time to commit to the sport blends to form a rare "perfect storm" of ingredients for success. In the age to come, I fear they will be non-existent. The art will be lost. I wanted to commit what I know to print before the art is gone and I am gone.

I would just add one candle of hope to this worrisome picture. A few Americans still hold a passion for the outdoors in their hearts. If you are one of those, I would just encourage you to ease your foot off the pedal of success pursuit just a bit and take the time to not only share God's creation with your kids, but do so at a pace they can enjoy as much as you. It honestly matters little what you take when they are young. They just want to be out there with their moms and dads.

And one more thing. Before you whip out your pen or e-mail client to lambaste me about being such a greedy hunter who should have left some deer in the woods for others to enjoy ...save your ink. The herd where I hunt has steadily increased every year of the thirty-five years I have been after them. The state of Alabama's herd has increased from 800,000 in the late 1960s to well over two million whitetails today. We have nearly as many whitetails as we do people! There are plenty for us all if you know where to get and go there when the conditions are right. That is why I'm sharing what I know with you today.

Hunting Ethics

There is nothing difficult about the gospel message to understand. Good hunting ethics are like the gospel of Jesus Christ ...easy to talk about, easy to understand, but a hard message for the human heart. No matter how you talk about your views of right and wrong, children easily see through any veil of hypocrisy.

My son and I were hunting at a commercial lodge when he was about four or five years old. The lodge owner had told us we could shoot pretty much anything, but to be careful not to shoot a button buck. About sundown a single deer entered the far corner of the field we were watching. I glassed it and confirmed it was a doe. Wanting him to experience some degree of success, I took the shot and climbed down to cross the field. When we got to the deer, it was a small button. I pulled the deer into the weeds and started back to the stand. Dust trailed behind me. I climbed up and encouragingly said, "Don't sweat it, Dust. We'll see another one." As I sat there, the agony of such foolishness began to gnaw at my conscience. Without taking my eye off the field, I finally said, "Dust, this isn't right. We have to go get the deer. We can't lie to the landowner." Then one of the most painful moments of life flooded my eyes with tears. I looked down at Dust, and tears were streaming down his cheeks. He had been crushed that his dad was going to lie to the lodge owner. He hadn't said a word. We climbed back down and walked across the field. When we really scrutinized the deer, it had been a young doe all along. I've been pretty careful to stick to the game laws with and without my kids present, but this time when I dropped my guard, my son was there to see it. What a stupid thing for a dad to do.

I mentioned earlier that one of the most enjoyable aspects of hunting the commercial hunting lodges was the opportunity to talk with other hunters. Folks who can afford to frequent these places are often successful, thought-provoking individuals. One of the subjects that frequently finds its way into the conversation is that of the animal rights activism. This causes the thoughtful person to take pause and consider the true ethics of hunting. Is it really okay to kill another animal? I think these folks ask a valid question. So what is the answer? I would approach this perplexing question from the same angle I approach all vexing questions. Scripture. What does the God who put it all into place think? Two ideas come to light in most any discussion with an animal rights activist. First, I have never met one who would even claim to be a Christian believer. In addition, I have never met an animal rights activist who was not a pro-abortionist. It strikes me as quite odd that one's ethics take such a high plain for a cockroach or a mouse or a dog, but can't seem to muster the guts to conjure even a sliver of passion for a defenseless human life, often snuffed out for the most trivial of reasons. Some, even during the process of being born! So from the perspective of these arguments, it would seem one must simply abandon any element of Christian belief in order to take up this defense. But again, it matters not one whit to me what the pagan may think of the morality of any act. What position has our Lord Jesus Christ taken on the subject of animal life and human life? That is where my confidence will lie.

From early in the scene of human existence, God has made it pretty clear where he stands. When Adam and Eve stepped away from his plan and rebelled, mankind entered a fallen and sinful world. Before that, I suspect there was little, if any, reason to hunt or even consider it. But in a fallen world, God Himself changed the rules by which we would live for our benefit. Adam had pieced together some pitiful fig leaves in a feeble effort to hide his newly noticed condition. God, not Adam and not Eve, went out and did what? Genesis 3:21: "And the Lord God made clothing from animal skins for Adam and his wife." [nlt] Now, let's face it. God put together a pretty vast and complex cosmos during the entire creation process. Why did he choose to take an animal's life to make clothes for these two miserable creatures who had so disappointed him? I don't know. He didn't say. But if he had wanted to make the clothes from some other material, I would think he had a lot of options at his disposal. He just left it to our imagination. However, it would seem that God never does anything without purpose. He is a God of order and balance and reason. Always. So, I suspect he was simply teaching Adam and Eve about what lay ahead...that he had made the animals in such a way as to serve a purpose for humanity. He makes no mistakes, wastes no effort, and commits no sins. Therefore, in my mind, the taking of an animal's life, whether it be a cockroach or a polar bear, is simply not a moral event. Nor is it a moral act. There is no right and wrong involved. It is what it is, nothing more, nothing less.

I won't belabor the point, but to just follow this thought on through Scripture a piece: Exodus 39:34 says: "the tent coverings of tanned ram skins and fine goatskin leather; the inner curtain to shield the Ark"; [nlt] God had Moses and Aaron use animal skins to make the tent used for his worship. He used animal skins to shield the ark of the covenant for his people. Noah, Abraham, Moses and a host of others throughout Scripture are directed specifically by God to sacrifice animals as an offering that were to represent a foreshadow of the ultimate sacrifice that was to come in Jesus Christ.

But what does Scripture have to say about taking animals by hunting? Genesis 25:27 describes Isaac's offspring, Jacob and Esau: "The boys grew up, and Esau became a skillful hunter, a man of the open country, while Jacob was a quiet man, staying among the tents." [niv]

Although one must sort of read between the lines here, the references to Esau indicated that God had decided before the boys were born that Esau was not going to be in his favor. Malachi 1:2–3 says: "'Was not Esau Jacob's brother?' the LORD says. 'Yet I have loved Jacob, but Esau I have hated, and I have turned his mountains into a wasteland and left his inheritance to the desert jackals.'" [niv] For reasons not clear in Scripture, God had decided Esau would become a great nation, but he would still always fail to be in God's favor. Was this because he was a hunter? Did Esau's passion for the outdoors and hunting cause God's disfavor? It did not. Romans 9:13–16 explains,

> Just as it is written: "Jacob I loved, but Esau I hated." What then shall we say? Is God unjust? Not at all! For he says to Moses, "I will have mercy on whom I have mercy, and I will have compassion on whom I have compassion." It does not, therefore, depend on man's desire or effort, but on God's mercy. [niv]

Just as with our own justification before God, this mercy is a matter handled by Christ once on the cross, just as it was with Esau and Jacob. Esau was here to serve a purpose in God's plan for his people, and this was decided before Esau and Jacob were born. It had nothing to do with his hunting. Again, we see that hunting is a moral nonevent before our Creator.

God seems most often to be more focused upon the motives for our actions rather than the acts themselves. There are no mentions of morality related to hunting. The only mention of animal cruelty is noted only when just that is happening. Take Balaam beating his donkey for example, in Numbers 22:32:

> The angel of the Lord asked him, "Why have you beaten your donkey these three times? I have come here to oppose you because your path is a reckless one before me. The donkey saw me and turned away from me these three times. If she had not turned away, I would certainly have killed you by now, but I would have spared her."
> [niv]

In the beginning, before Satan had enticed us into sin, the arrangements went something like this: Genesis 1:20–31:

> And God said, "Let the water teem with living creatures, and let birds fly above the earth across the expanse of the

sky." So God created the great creatures of the sea and every living and moving thing with which the water teems, according to their kinds, and every winged bird according to its kind. And God saw that it was good. God blessed them and said, "Be fruitful and increase in number and fill the water in the seas, and let the birds increase on the earth." And there was evening, and there was morning—the fifth day. And God said, "Let the land produce living creatures according to their kinds: livestock, creatures that move along the ground, and wild animals, each according to its kind." And it was so. God made the wild animals according to their kinds, the livestock according to their kinds, and all the creatures that move along the ground according to their kinds. And God saw that it was good. Then God said, "Let us make man in our image, in our likeness, and let them rule over the fish of the sea and the birds of the air, over the livestock, over all the earth, and over all the creatures that move along the ground."[niv]

Basically, there was no need for animals to eat each other or for man to eat animals. Plants formed the food chain basis for both. But that all changed after man's fall into sin. And God adjusted his creation accordingly. There became a host of reasons for animals to be used for food, for sacrifice, for beasts of burden, for battle, for transportation, etc. God addresses this again in Acts 11:5–11, where he makes it clear to Peter that the arrangements have changed yet again. The sacrificial system is passing away and that now, he may eat anything that God provides on the earth for food: He "saw something like a large sheet being let down from heaven by its four corners, and it came down to where I was. I looked into it and saw four footed animals of the earth, wild beasts, reptiles, and birds of the air. Then I heard a voice telling me, 'Get up, Peter. Kill and eat.'" [niv] God simply does not direct someone to sin. Period.

Nature's Way Out

Now, let's approach this idea of animal rights activism and the anti-hunter from yet another angle. We, as hunters, are portrayed as uncivilized and heartless when we suddenly end the life of a whitetail. Okay. Did you ever wonder how a whitetail's life ends at the hands of the anti-hunter's revered nature? Did you really think they just wander off into the forest, lie down peacefully by a quiet stream, and pass into a blissful afterlife? If so, you need to wake up to a harsh reality. This is utter nonsense.

The most common predator across most of the whitetail's habitat (other than man) is the coyote. A coyote is an intelligent, but ruthless hunter. However, he is also a fairly small animal. Unlike a lion or grizzly, he cannot snap a whitetail's neck with a single bite. He relentlessly pursues any whitetail in the herd that shows any signs of weakness or exhaustion. Once he gets close, he typically, in conjunction with others in the pack, will hamstring the deer putting him on the ground. Still his teeth are typical canines and, as such, cannot break through the thick hide of the whitetail. So, unhampered by the social stigmata typical of human emotions, he goes for the thin tissue around the deer's anus. Here, he can break through the hide. He starts to eat the deer working his way into the muscle of the hindquarters ...all while the whitetail agonizes through the pain, he can no longer escape. The deer is literally eaten alive, one bite at a time. He bleats. He jerks. He scuffles. He does all he can to escape. But the coyote is a small animal. The whitetail is eaten slowly over a period of hours. He bears no remorse toward the whitetail. He feels no compassion. He does not hate the whitetail. He is simply a wild animal with no abstract thought. I am not relating to you here what I have read from a biological textbook folks. I have seen this scene play out many times in the real world of the whitetail. Nature wields a brutal, merciless, savage, and cruel end to any whitetail's life that falls victim to his common predator.

But wait. This is not the end. How do whitetails otherwise die naturally in the wild? Disease is likely the second most common cause of death for the whitetail. There are several protozoans, bacteria, and a few prions that take down these majestic animals. All do so over hours to days, slowly weakening the animal. If he is so lucky as to avoid an always nearby coyote, he is left to slowly starve, dehydrate, and finally fall to the ground where he often lays for days with fever, diarrhea, and muscle aches. He may seize. He may lose his vision and lay in the darkness wondering when the merciful coyote will show up to finish him off. But his death is virtually always a slow and agonizing one.

The third most common method of demise, at least for the males in the herd, is that of fighting until one of several things happens. Two mature bucks often fight to the death. They frequently lock their antlers together, and hence they stay until they both starve over a period of days to weeks. Many, many examples of this have been confirmed in nature. Often a single emaciated animal is found by hunters dragging the carcass of his decaying opponent. More often, though, one of the beasts will punch through his opponent's side with an antler in the process of fighting. A lung or gut may be punctured and from this, infection sets in. The animal becomes sick, feverish, weak, and over days to a week or two, dies an agonizing death...again, if the coyote doesn't find him first!

For the females in the herd, there is always fawning, the process of giving birth. As most women will attest, this is no cakewalk even under the best of anesthesia. For the whitetail, it is often a slow bleed into weakness and death, particularly for those young does in the herd. The birthing process is a tough one for them just as it is for the primiparous human female.

For the fortunate whitetail, there is one seemingly civil way to pass away these days, and a quite common one at that...being hit by an automobile. Even here, more than half the incidents of whitetail death is not instantaneous. As often as not, the animal limps into the woods with a broken leg, fractured spine, or a cracked skull...but still alive and hurting. If he's lucky, he may bleed to death within a few hours from internal organ damage. If not, and he makes it until dark, the trusty coyote will be on patrol through the nighttime hours.

The Hunter's Way Out

Now, let's be honest and contrast nature's way of controlling the whitetail herd with that of the modern hunter. We have two favorite weapons, the bow and arrow and the centerfire or black powder rifle. There has been a plethora of research done on these methods of taking whitetails as well as many large African game animals, and the results have been cataloged and published widely. When a modern razor-equipped broadhead passes through a whitetail at speeds in the range of 200 to 300 feet per second, pushed by a tiny carbon-spined arrow, the response of the whitetail is so predictable we have come to expect it. He bounces a few yards and stops to look back. He acts as though an acorn hit him on the back. More often than not, he will walk slowly away, only to wobble and fall to his instant death within about twenty seconds! He rarely covers more than thirty yards. Many, many times, I have punched through a feeding whitetail with a broadhead and had him go back to feeding within a few seconds. Stuff is falling from the trees in his habitat all the time as the wind loosens branches, acorns, blooms, and other debris from the canopy above. He responds, but is rarely frightened. If he were in pain, he would clearly not return to feeding. A whitetail does not feed when he is disturbed in the least. Death is more often than not, complete in less than twenty seconds. For the centerfire and black powder rifle, death is even more instantaneous and humane, generally occurring within about five to fifteen seconds.

So we have established that the taking of an animal's life is morally a non-event. We have made it gruesomely clear that the anti-hunter's approach of leaving it to nature is anything but empathetic and compassionate. We have also established that the hunter's methods of ending an animal's life is quick, painless and quite humane. Mishaps do occur, but they are the exception and beat nature's alternatives hands down ...morally, statistically, and humanely.

Last of a Species

I would like to put to rest one more of our pagan society's neuroses about the animal kingdom, and that is the idea of trying to save every species left on the planet. The decay of God's creation is an unavoidable result of sin having entered the world. It is not going to stop until the end has come. I am not advocating that we recklessly end any species' existence. However, to spend billions of dollars and place mankind at risk of poverty and loss as a result of trying to save a minnow, mouse, or a tweety bird is simply ridiculous. To really flesh this out, I have included an additional chapter to follow that should make it clear where I stand on God and animals and life in general. It involves some truly original thought and some philosophical, "deep weeds" if you will. So brace yourself.

Some ten or so years back, I was attending an annual meeting of our Christian denomination (Presbyterian Church in America), the General Assembly. The PCA, as it is commonly referred to, takes a pretty conservative view of Scripture, and as such, for a pastor to be ordained into the denomination to teach and preach, he must agree before the Presbytery that he accepts a literal view of the account of creation as described in Genesis. At this particular General Assembly, some 2000 teaching and ruling elders had assembled and this issue of just how to interpret the creation account was hotly debated for several days running. The leaders were clearly divided, though the final decision was to preserve the conservative, "literal" view. But some good people came down on both sides of the issue. I had come to a very clear solution concerning this apparent dilemma several years prior, but had never really verbalized it to anyone other than my family and local church leaders. And, to be honest, just grasping the concept behind it requires a basic understanding of some pretty serious analytical math and physics. During the drive home from Dallas, Texas, to Tuscaloosa,

Alabama, I spent about ten hours reducing the following quite unorthodox insight to paper.

The Story of Creation

Science vs. the Bible... the First Six Days

The works of many of history's most celebrated scientists and mathematicians were not recognized until these great men had been dead for many years. Examples include Newton, Pascal, Copernicus, "http://www.kepler.arc.nasa.gov/johannes.html" Kepler, Planck, and most recently, Einstein. Albert Einstein, however, did enjoy some notoriety during his lifetime, predominantly from a part of his Special Theory of Relativity, introduced in 1905, which led to the discovery of the relationship between energy and matter, the famous E=mc2. The practical application of this theory ultimately brought an end to the Second World War and hence ushered in the age of the harnessing of nuclear energy.

Practical Relativity

However, Einstein's General Theory of Relativity introduced in 1915 received much less attention and in fact, has gone largely unnoticed by all but the most academic of physicists, mathematicians and post graduate educators (with the possible exception of the eight million people who purchased a copy of Stephen Hawking's A Brief History of Time). Nevertheless its (relativity's) elaboration contains perhaps the most practical application of biblical truth since Kepler's discovery of the true structure of our solar system, dispelling thousands of years of misunderstanding of the Bible. Unlike Kepler whose work stemmed directly from his staunch belief in the inerrancy of Scripture, Einstein was unable to reconcile the pain and suffering evident in the world to an omnipotent, omniscient, and loving God. This led him to reject the notion of an expanding universe until the last few years of his life. His equations pointed to an expanding universe, but throughout his life he applied a "universal expansion constant" which corrected his equations to represent a static (eternal) universe. As the data mounted pointing unmistakably toward the truth of this universal expansion (hence demanding a beginning, i.e., Creation), Einstein finally conceded, "This was the biggest blunder of my life, when "http://www.pbs.org/wgbh/aso/databank/entries/b. Edwin Hubble proved without a shadow of doubt the expansion of the universe.

Few today would debate the fact that Einstein's theories have become widely accepted by the scientific community next to the laws of nature defined by Newton, Galileo, and Kepler. Even fewer, though, realize or even know about the second part of his theory describing the relationship between time, space, velocity (Special Relativity), and gravity (General Relativity). From our point of reference on the earth, the passing of time has a rather absolute and unchanging appearance. But then, so does our velocity. From our viewpoint along the surface of the earth, we have no sensation whatever that we are moving; yet we are swishing along through space at a smooth 1000 miles per hour as the earth's surface rotates on its central axis. More amazingly, we travel around the sun on the earth's orbit at an astounding 67,000 miles per hour! Yet, from our viewpoint, we sense no evidence of this velocity of motion.

The Universe Is Expanding (Hence, a Beginning!)

An overview of Einstein's theory shows us that the passing of time is, in fact, relative to ...(1) the velocity from one's current viewpoint (or inertial reference frame) in the universe and (2) the gravity near that point in the universe.The math behind this relationship is not quite so simple as

E=mc2, but suffice it to say that the greater the velocity and/or the mass (and resultant gravity), the more compressed the passing of time will be (*when viewed from a given reference frame*). This idea of time being relative (dependent upon our frame of reference in the universe) is profoundly difficult for us to come to grips with. It is most counter intuitive. Yet we know from a variety of scientifically confirmed observations such as the absolute temperature of the universe in black space (2.73 degrees Kelvin) as evidenced by the omnipresent cosmic background radiation (that ever present time clock of radiation left over from the "big bang" of Creation), and the redshift of distant stars in galaxies beyond the Milky Way, that the universe is expanding at a constant rate. These facts demand that all observers must view their own special version of time, depending upon their reference frame in the time-space continuum. Viewing this seeming paradox from another angle, it demands that the passing of time is relative to local gravity and/or one's velocity through that time-space fabric.

Let's consider a common application of this principle from daily living that each of us likely takes for granted, our current GPS satellite system. If the effect that relativity has on the passing of time in just one day were not taken into account in the mathematical formulae used to triangulate with light waves a specific location on the earth's surface, the precision of the positioning system would be off by several miles! This is because of the error in distance interjected because the speed of light remains the same for all observers in any reference frame. This means the passing of time on the earth's surface is noticeably faster (because of gravity's effect on the passing of time) than that observed at the satellite's location in space above the earth's surface.

An even simpler practical conception of this theory's relevance was revealed when a group of scientists placed two atomic clocks, one atop a tall water tower and another at its base. According to Einstein's General Theory of Relativity, the clock closest to the gravitational field of the earth should run more slowly (i.e. Time is moving faster). And indeed it did!

Time Is Relative!

Remembering that when the universe was younger (say, perhaps, during the first few days after its creation), it was much more compact. Heavenly bodies, including the earth, were in much closer proximity to each other. Hence, had we been present (as was our Creator) to observe the passing of those first six days from a viewpoint (inertial reference frame) on the surface of an earth surrounded by the almost unimaginably large mass (and gravitational forces) of this compact universe, the passing of those first six days would have been much, much faster compared to our inertial reference frame (frame of reference) on the surface of the earth at its velocity and location in space *today* (although the passing of time then would have appeared exactly the same as today *from that reference frame*). Said another way, comparing those first six days to the relative length of time it takes for the passing of "six days" today on the earth, approximately 15.7 billion years would have passed ...*during those first six days* when viewed from today's reference frame! Therefore, as you can see, there really is no conflict between the geologic age of the earth (and the universe) as determined by modern science and that of the biblical account of Creation in Genesis. It did indeed all occur in six days, defined as morning and evening, the passing of one day just as Genesis states. Our Creator, the designer and sustainer of all that exists, views this universe with its inherent time, space, mass, and physical laws obviously from outside its relative time. Hence, the profound revelation from his Word, Psalm 90:4,"For a thousand years in your sight are like a day that has just gone by, or like a watch in the night," and 2 Peter 3:8, "But do not forget this one thing, dear friends: With the Lord a day is like a thousand years, and a thousand years are like a day" (niv).

Evolution Is Not the Answer

Now, don't flinch and leave this discussion thinking that I am drawing the conclusion that just because the earth appears geologically to be very old, that I am somehow trying to leave a crack in the door through which to drive the truck of macroevolution. Quite the contrary, just because the earth appears very old, we need not conclude that God was confined to the use of macroevolution (the gradual generation of new and more complex life forms from earlier and more simple life forms) in order to generate the vast array of life forms we see on the earth today, nor those evident from the fossil record. Many Christian scientists today have bought into this idea of Creation. However, the fossil record fits the order, type, timing, pattern (in phases), and magnitude of plant and animal life as they appeared on the scene in Genesis far more precisely than it does that of gradual macroevolution. The Bible and the geologic and fossil records agree that the strata of plant and animal life suddenly burst onto the scene in clear and distinct phases rather than by way of a gradual process such as macroevolution. In fact, if you do the math, the Genesis account so precisely fits that of the scientific record that one must wonder why all the fuss about rejecting it. It is as though the earth was finely tuned to support the life that was to come during each phase. Following the Creation event, as the earth would become ripe for life of a particular type, God would bring it into being in tremendous phases amidst a perfectly tuned ecosystem.

Six Days of Creation: The correlation between the geologic and biblical accounts are really quite staggering when compared.

From Gods view at the beginning of creation looking forward six days	From our view looking back in time using our frame of reference on the earth's position in the cosmos *today*	Approximate years before Adam at the start of each of the six days of creation looking back in time using our frame of reference on the earth's position in the cosmos *today*	The Biblical account	The Geologic and Fossil records
Day one... 24 hrs	lasted approximately 8 billion years	The day began 15.7 billion years ago	Initial creation w/the creation of light (Genesis 1:1-5	The beginning of the Big Bang
Day two... 24 hrs	lasted approximately 4 billion years	The day began 7.6 billion years ago	The firmament forms (Genesis 1:6-8)	The stars including our sun and earth form
Day three.. 24 hrs	lasted approximately 2 billion years	The day began 3.7 billion years ago	Oceans and dry land and first plant life appear (Genesis 1:9-13)	liquid water appears with the immediate presence of simple plants such as bacteria and algae

Day four... 24 hrs	lasted approximately 1 billion years	The day began 1.7 billion years ago	The sun, moon, and stars become visible in the heavens (Genesis 1:14-19)	Pre-Cambrian Age: The earth's atmosphere becomes transparent and photosynthesis of the early plant life forms oxygen rich atmosphere
Day five... 24 hrs	lasted approximately 500 million years	The day began 800 million years ago	First animal life including fish, reptiles and winged animals appear (Genesis 1:20-23)	Cambrian Age: The first complex organisms including fish, birds and reptiles appear in the fossil record. (No mammalian land animals have shown up in the fossil record to this point.)
Day six... 24 hrs	lasted approximately 250 million years and ended approximately 6000 years ago	The day began 250 million years ago and likely ended approximately 6000 years ago	Land animals, mammals and humans appear (Genesis 1:24-31)	Mesozoic Age: modern trees, land animals, mammals and near the end of this day, man appears.

A Practical Insight

One afternoon not long ago, my wife and I were walking along a gravel country road when I reached down and picked up a nearly perfectly spherical sandstone rock. I showed it to her and we speculated upon how nature must have caused it to be so round. A bit further down the same road, I picked up a five-eighths-inch hexagonal head steel bolt with a lock washer and a hexagonal nut attached. I passed it to her and said, "Amazing how nature could form two such different formations" (referring to the round rock and the bolt assembly).

She looked at me wryly and said, "Have you been drinking the cooking sherry?"

Had this bolt/washer/nut assembly crashed into one of our space stations from distant space, anyone, virtually regardless of their position on the existence of God, would have concluded that intelligent design was inherently obvious in the bolt/washer/nut assembly.

Yet, we look at the order and staggering complexity inherent within the human genome and the end products of its templating in the formation of a human organism and conclude that there is no evidence of intelligent design here? Give me a break! If we took the basic ingredients of a Boeing 747 jumbo jet and brought them into close proximity within a large cauldron of molten elements and compounds, what do you suppose would be the mathematical likelihood of a new 747 forming by random chance over extreme periods of time without outside influence from intelligent design? On the surface, the question seems preposterous. Yet, this is the very logic we use to conclude that random mathematical chance produced entities far more complex than a 747 in the process of natural Darwinian selection working through the macro evolutionary process. How desperate we are to reject God!

Even if we had not been given the Scriptures to reveal God's special revelation to us in nature, one would have to engage a really vivid imagination to buy into the idea of macroevolution. Perhaps you have never really read Charles Darwin's Origin of Species. It represents a compelling argument favoring gradual evolution if, and only if, you have first completely rejected any possibility of Creation. Hence, the very objectivity on which the evolutionist bases his claims goes up in smoke.

God, in fact, pointed out that the Creation speaks so clearly in favor of his existence that we have no excuse for rejecting him based upon its general revelation. Psalm 19:1–2: "The heavens are telling of the glory of God; And their expanse is declaring the work of his hands. Day to day pours forth speech, And night to night reveals knowledge." Romans 1:20: "For since the creation of the world his invisible attributes, his eternal power and divine nature, have been clearly seen, being understood through what has been made, so that they are without excuse" (nasb). When science seems to contradict the Bible, we can have confidence in the Scriptures' unfailing truth not because we are dogmatic and follow a blind faith. On the contrary, if we open our eyes in a truly unbiased fashion, science will always reveal the truth of Scripture.

Stop for a moment and think about this. If this macroevolutionary machine is such an efficient producer of plant and animal life, just how many new species have burst onto the scene in the last few thousand years? Don't you think that if it were able to produce millions upon millions of species over the geologic ages, that we would have seen evidence of at least one new specie roll off the assembly line every few thousand years? Yet there is not one. All we have is this feeble link of similarity buried in the fossil record of the earth's strata, and a few mutations and genetic drift within a single specie.

Now, how many species have become extinct in your lifetime? Hundreds! What did the Scriptures predict about the continual decay of Creation after the fall? Romans 8:21: "That the creation itself will be liberated from its bondage to decay and brought into the glorious freedom of the children of God" (niv). Genesis 3:16–19:

> To the woman he said, "I will greatly
> multiply Your pain in childbirth, In
> pain you shall bring forth children; Yet
> your desire shall be for your husband,
> And he shall rule over you." Then to
> Adam he said, "Because you have
> listened to the voice of your wife, and

have eaten from the tree about which I commanded you, saying, 'You shall not eat from it'; Cursed is the ground because of you; In toil you shall eat of it all the days of your life. Both thorns and thistles it shall grow for you; And you shall eat the plants of the field; By the sweat of your face You shall eat bread, Till you return to the ground, Because from it you were taken; For you are dust, And to dust you shall return." (nasb)

A Word of Caution

For those of you Christian believers who find yourselves wanting to believe such rational logic as this, but also are cautious about leaning on one's own understanding, I applaud your discernment and caution not to be swayed by every new idea the wind blows in. But I also ask that you remember the stories of our number who came before us guarding the truth of Scripture. When "http://www.blupete.com" Giordano Bruno, a follower of "http://www.blupete.com/Literature/Biographies" Copernicus and a contemporary of Galileo, ventured to even suggest that the earth might not be the center of the universe, well meaning but obviously overzealous church clergy took him out back and promptly burned him at the stake for such heresy! Sensing what was coming, Galileo himself escaped the clergy barely with his life after he was forced to publicly renounce his own theories concerning planetary motion.

When the Scriptures use phrases like "the four corners of the earth," "take the earth by the edges," and "from the ends of the earth," we must be careful not to assume these literary forms are meant, in their context, to portray geologic, cosmic or astronomic insights. We have nothing to fear in believing the inerrant Bible. When we see the findings of science in seeming contradiction to the Scriptures, just relax, be patient, and learn. Our Creator is sovereign over all he has made. Science can ultimately prove nothing less nor anything more.

A Comforting Thought

There is just one more point about this relativity issue I would like you to consider. Honestly, did you ever wonder just how it is that God, through Jesus Christ's death on the cross, atoned for the sins of not just those who came after him, but for those who lived before him? Does that not strike you as a bit odd? However, in view of general relativity as Einstein presented it in 1915, and certainly as we understand it today in the twenty-first century, the event of Christ's atoning work on the cross does not bind God to any time-space absolutes. God is at work from outside our "inertial reference frame" (our point of reference in the created time-space continuum). Therefore, this event has no time constraints from God's perspective. He is free by his very design of the universe with its time-space elements to perform outside its limits an act of eternal consequences and value. I find that awfully reassuring.

I have read and reread books on this subject by intense, brilliant, discerning scientists like Stephen Hawking, Ph.D., Donald Chittick, Ph.D., Hugh Ross, Ph.D., Gerald Schroeder, Ph.D. Albert Einstein, and a host of others including textbooks on physics, organic and physical chemistry, and quantum mechanics. Each has excellent points to make and some of these guys might well disagree with my conclusions. The real truth of the matter is that I do not know for certain whether I am correct about the effect gravity has on the passing of time with respect to those first six days outlined in Genesis. However, I believe the factual data I used to arrive at these conclusions is solid and that the concept does not violate Scripture and is easily verified by modern science. In fact, they both quite nicely confirm it.

My overarching and compelling reason for even entering this debate rests in a heartfelt hope of bringing Christian brothers together...to give us some common ground upon which we might assemble peacefully, yet continue to expand our knowledge of this incredible Creation.

This season when you pick up your bow and stroll off into a patch of hardwoods shedding their amber leaves in a cool autumn breeze, remember what I have said here. Look up into the heavens and know that we are here for a reason...to honor and worship the God who made it all possible, and to love those down the street and across the oceans with a passion that would make him proud.

About the Author

Dr. Bob Sheppard grew up on a farm in Alabama, born in 1950, the son of tenant farmers. He descended from a long line of fishermen and hunters. He began a writing career in the outdoor field during his years of medical school and residency, and became a staff writer for an Alabama based magazine called the Alabama Sportsman (later to become one of Game & Fish Publication's periodicals, Alabama Game & Fish). Over the next fifteen years, he placed articles in Outdoor Life, Field & Stream, Sports Afield, Bowhunter Magazine, Harris Publication's books and annuals, Deer & Deer Hunting, Progressive Farmer, Southern Outdoors, Game & Fish Publications, and a host of others. In 1979 he began instructing in a series of bowhunting schools held at commercial hunting lodges across the South. These have become the nation's oldest continuous line of outdoor skills schools in existence.

Read more at <u>A. Robert Sheppard, M.D.'s site</u>.

Made in the USA
Columbia, SC
16 December 2018